WRITING HANDBOOKS

Writing
DIALOGUE
FOR SCRIPTS

SECOND EDITION

RIB DAVIS

A & C Black • London

Second edition 2003
Reprinted 2005
First published 1998
A & C Black Publishers Limited
37 Soho Square, London W1D 3QZ
www.acblack.com

© 2003, 1998 Rib Davis

ISBN 0–7136–6380–4

A CIP catalogue record for this book is
available from the British Library.

A & C Black uses paper produced with elemental chlorine-free pulp,
harvested from managed sustainable forests.

Typeset in 10/12 pt Sabon
Printed and bound in Great Britain by
Creative Print and Design (Wales), Ebbw Vale

WRITING HANDBOOKS

Writing
DIALOGUE
FOR SCRIPTS

SECOND EDITION

Books in the 'Writing Handbooks' series

Other books for writers

Introduction

Most dramatic scripts consist mainly of dialogue. Of course, there are also stage directions – a line, a paragraph or at the very most a page or two – and an eccentric writer might even digress to talk about the meaning of the text, but generally a script will consist predominantly of dialogue. This applies whatever medium the script is intended for, whether theatre, radio, film or television. In film or television there may be whole sequences – perhaps held together by music – in which there is no dialogue at all, while in the theatre, too, there may be sections dominated by visual action; but generally it is the dialogue that cements a script, that holds it together. This book takes a microscope to that cement, and then uses the findings to provide not only some insights into how dialogue works, but also a better understanding of how to go about writing it.

Here we set out, then, to study the writing of dialogue as it exists across the script media. There are of course differences of approach and usage from one medium to another, but the types of dialogue used in each medium have much more in common with each other than they have differences.

Yet dialogue in scripts is utterly entwined with the other elements of the work – the characterisation, the plot, the action, the structure, the visual effects, the music... How is it possible to extricate the dialogue from all this and talk about it separately? It can be done, but with some difficulty. In his book *Aspects of the Novel*, E.M. Forster noted the problem when trying to disentangle 'story' from other elements of novel-writing; yet he does conclude that somehow one might pull out what he calls this 'tapeworm' of story, even if other things tend to cling on to it. My experience is very similar. It is possible to talk about dialogue, even if along the way one has continually to refer to all the other bits and pieces that one finds still attached to it. After all, without a plot, characterisation

1

and the rest, dialogue alone is of very little use to us. It always has to be placed in its context.

There is a great deal of advice for the scriptwriter in this book, and, after the opening chapters which look at how conversation works in 'real life', that advice is very much linked in with examples from real scripts. These extracts are analysed in some detail, as there is much for the scriptwriter to learn from the example set by others. Most of the extracts chosen are from scripts of the twentieth and twenty-first centuries, but there are also a few quotations from earlier times, since in some respects the modern writer can learn as much from Shakespeare and Jonson as from Stoppard and Tarantino. In addition I have used extracts from a number of my own scripts, not because I believe they are in the same league as the work of the writers mentioned above, but simply because I do have a very clear idea of what I was intending to achieve in my own scripts.

In one well-known 200-page book on screenwriting, just half a page is devoted to dialogue. The author presents four purposes of dialogue, pointing out that many writers find dialogue the most difficult part of their work, but then adding that good dialogue will come with experience. While this attitude seems inadequate to the point of being cavalier, it is true that to some extent the writing of dialogue may be 'caught rather than taught'. Writers who have 'a good ear for dialogue' – those who pick up the inflections of the speech of others with apparently effortless ease – obviously have a head start. However, just as a musician who may not have perfect pitch may nevertheless be trained to identify and notate harmonies, rhythms and melodies – and then may also be trained in how to use them in composition – so may the writer be assisted in learning how to listen to dialogue and how to write it. We can *learn* what to consciously listen out for in everyday speech – all the subtle ways in which it functions – and we can learn too how to use dialogue in scripts most effectively.

Ultimately, of course, a writer learns most by the hard road of experience, trial and error (particularly error), but this book should at least point out some of the pot-holes and cul-de-sacs – and perhaps a few bypasses – in advance, and should help to make the journey a little less painful.

1. How Do We Talk?

Writing and speaking

When we are scripting dialogue we are, of course, scripting speech. That speech is nearly always fictional – it is hardly ever the exact words that anyone has actually said on any specific occasion. Yet although there are many styles of scripted dialogue, whatever style is used it will always relate in some way to how people talk in 'real life'. The writer, then, needs to have a very clear understanding of how speech and conversation work. So, although most of this book concentrates upon aspects of the *scripting* of dialogue, in this chapter the focus is on the raw material – the ways in which we speak in real life.

We tend to take speech for granted. We want to say things, so we say them; we need to listen to people's replies, so we do. And that's about it. Generally, we don't think too much about it. Unlike written language, with its rules about clauses and punctuation, speech is not generally taught, but rather it is caught, and as a result we tend to under-estimate just how complex and varied it actually is. For many of us, it is only when we try to reproduce speech – as dialogue in a script – that we realise it is not quite as straightforward as we had assumed. Of course, there may be very good reasons for a scriptwriter *not* to reproduce in its entirety language as we commonly speak it – and we will come on to many of these reasons later – but that does not detract from the fact that it is important to be aware of how conversation actually functions before setting out to script dialogue.

Spoken language is very different from written language. Even written language which is relatively informal in tone (such as that in this book) is still a very long way from language as we use it in everyday conversation. So what, exactly, is the difference? The basic point is that conversational language, unlike written language, is a mess, though a mess that we are all entirely used to dealing with.

3

Chatting together, for example, we will often leave sentences unfinished, or we will realise half-way through that there is a better way of putting something, so after a false start we begin again.

> We came along the – it was on the A27 and we caught up with them near Brighton...

We are improvising, and revising our thoughts – or at least our way of expressing them – as we go along.

Running repairs to speech

This improvising doesn't seem strange at all, but perfectly natural. Indeed, the individual who speaks without any hesitations or revisions whatsoever will probably speak slowly and may well have a tendency to be pedantic; and they might well be seen as rather tedious, or at least lacking in spontaneity. Conversation normally does have a strong element of *spontaneity*, of *improvising*, of *changing things as we go along*. Written language, on the other hand, has usually had these elements ironed out in the drafting and re-drafting. With the exception of a formal speech, such as in the House of Commons or at a business dinner (where incidentally the speech normally starts life as something written anyway), there is usually no drafting or re-drafting of spoken language.

To go back to the car trip example, we are being told about it verbally, not through written language, so it might continue in this way:

> ... caught up with them near Brighton, yeah, near Brighton. Terrible traffic, and pouring with rain. And it was getting dark by now, too. Could hardly make out which was their car.

Here we have one sentence without a main verb, another sentence without a subject, and a repetition which adds nothing new at all – yet when spoken it all sounds normal. On the page, however, it looks odd, since we are used to language on the page being neater, more controlled, more correct. The problem is that although dialogue is spoken, dialogue in scripts is at the same time written language – written language designed to be spoken – and in the process of putting the words down on to the page we may find ourselves tempted to tidy them up, to make them appear less awkward on paper. In other words, we may feel the urge to make written dialogue look more like the rest of written language. Thus, if the verbal report on the journey were part of a script, instead of the above we might write:

> The traffic was terrible and it was pouring with rain... We could hardly make out which was their car.

There is nothing wrong with this as a piece of dialogue. Many people on many occasions might well express themselves in this way; others on other occasions would speak in the first, less 'correct' way; while others again might speak in a manner somewhere between the two or, in stylistic terms, more extreme than either of them.

Interruptions and simultaneous speech

In conversation, the improvisation of speech not only leads to sentences often being unfinished or restarted, verbs, subjects or other parts of speech often being missed out and words or ideas being unnecessarily repeated; there is also all the messiness that arises from the fact that there is more than one person taking part. Talking together, *we continually interrupt and speak across each other*. We may have been taught that these things are not polite, but in fact we do them all the time, and very often they do not feel impolite at all. If when you speak you are listened to in silence until you have finished speaking, the effect can be a very awkward one – you can feel almost as though you were being interviewed, or it can seem that the listener is not interested, or doesn't understand, or perhaps is even irritated or bored. So very often the listener will interrupt with 'Yes...', 'Of course...', or 'Exactly the same happened to me...' to show at the very least that they are still listening, and hopefully also that they recognise the truth of what is being said. The listener may interrupt with 'No, I don't think so... ' if he or she disagrees, but even this interruption is not usually taken to be rude. Sometimes one of these interjections will just be a second or two of simultaneous speech, with the first speaker continuing, while at other points in the conversation the interruption will lead to the new speaker taking over so that the speeches of the two overlap for a few words. Very often we will anticipate when another person is coming to the end of what they want to say and, rather than wait for the very end, we will come in a second or two early. Usually this does not seem at all impolite; it is a perfectly normal element of everyday talk. When we write dialogue, however, this is another element which we might find ourselves perhaps unconsciously tidying up. Of course, a writer may have good reasons for doing just that (and more will be said about this in later chapters), but here we need to recognise that the raw material – everyday conversation – is more messy than we had probably appreciated and is certainly much messier than written dialogue, and that a major reason for this is the *interaction* between speakers.

One of the themes of David Mamet's extraordinary play *Oleana* is the difficulty experienced in genuinely communicating. The play begins with a phone call.

JOHN (*on phone*): And what about the land. (*Pause*) The land. And what about the land? (*Pause*) What about it? (*Pause*) No. I don't understand. Well, yes, I'm I'm... no, I'm sure it's signif... I'm sure it's significant. (*Pause*) Because it's significant to mmmmmm... did you call Jerry? (*Pause*) Because... no, no, no, no, no. What did they say... ? Did you speak to the *real* estate... where is she... ? Well, well, all right. Where are her notes? Where are the notes we took with her. (*Pause*) I thought you were? No. No, I'm sorry, I didn't mean that, I just thought that I saw you, when we were there... what...? I thought I saw you with a *pencil*. WHY NOW? is what I'm say... well, that's why I say "call Jerry." Well, I can't right now, be... no, I *didn't* schedule any... Grace: I *didn't*... I'm well aware... Look: Look. Did you call Jerry? Will you call Jerry... ? Because I can't now. I'll be there, I'm sure I'll be there in fifteen, in twenty. I intend to. No, we aren't *going* to lose the, we aren't *going* to lose the house. Look: Look, I'm not minimising it. The "easement." Did she say "easement"? (*Pause*) What did she *say*; is it a "term of art," are we bound by it... I'm sorry... (*Pause*) are: we: yes. *Bound* by ... Look: (*He checks his watch.*) before the other side *goes home*, all right? "a term of art." Because: that's right. (*Pause*) The yard for the boy. Well, that's the whole... Look: I'm going to meet you there... (*He checks his watch.*) Is the realtor there? All right, tell her to show you the basement again. Look at *this* because... Bec... I'm leaving in, I'm leaving in ten or fifteen... Yes. No, no, I'll meet you at the new... That's a good. If he

thinks it's nec... you tell Jerry to meet... All right? We *aren't*
going to lose the deposit. All right? I'm sure it's going to be...
(*Pause*) I hope so. (*Pause*) I love you, too. (*Pause*) I love you,
too. As soon as... I will.
(*He hangs up.*)

Phone calls are often poorly presented in scripts, with the person at
this end making artificial re-statements of the unheard speeches for
the benefit of the audience. But not here. Despite only hearing one
side of the conversation we gain the gist of the meaning – and feel
the tension of the situation – while at the same time we are aware
of all the general *messiness* of this verbal interaction. There are the
repetitions, the half-made sentences and even half-made words, the
misunderstandings and re-phrasings, the false starts and hesitations
and, above all, the overlappings and interruptions. This is dialogue
full of running repairs.

In the Mamet example, all the mess of conversation is written
into the dialogue itself. At one point in the play *Our Country's
Good*, Timberlake Wertenbaker comes up with a different
solution. In Scene Six, which involves no fewer than ten speaking
characters, rather than attempt to commit to paper all the overlaps
and simultaneities of speech which would occur, Wertenbaker
presents the main dialogue only – but invites improvisations from
the cast with the following stage direction:

> *It is late at night, the men have been drinking, tempers are high.
> They interrupt each other, overlap, make jokes under and over
> the conversation but all engage in it with the passion for
> discourse and thought of eighteenth-century man.*

More commonly, however, the messiness of dialogue is written into
the script, so a number of writers have developed particular styles
of presentation for interruptions and overlapping speech. Caryl
Churchill, for example, uses the slash, / , to indicate that at this
point the next speech starts; an asterisk, *, is used to match up the
point where a speech overlaps with another, when the two speeches
are not consecutive on the page; and finally, when a speech continues right across another speech, she simply leaves the first speech
adrift with no punctuation at all where the other speech begins,
and then continues it without an upper case start. All these are
present in the following extract from her play *Top Girls*. A group

of prominent women from various periods of history are in a restaurant together, looking at the menu, while the waitress stands next to them:

ISABELLA. Yes, I forgot all my Latin. But my father was the mainspring of my life and when he died I was so grieved. I'll have the chicken, please, / and the soup.
NIJO. Of course you were grieved. My father was saying his prayers and he dozed off in the sun. So I touched his knee to rouse him. 'I wonder what will happen,' he said, and then he was dead before he finished the sentence. / If he died saying
MARLENE. What a shock.
NIJO. his prayers he would have gone straight to heaven. / Waldorf salad.
JOAN. Death is the return of all creatures to God.
NIJO. I shouldn't have woken him.
JOAN. Damnation only means ignorance of the truth. I was always attracted by the teaching of John the Scot, though he was inclined to confuse / God and the world.
ISABELLA. Grief always overwhelmed me at the time.
MARLENE. What I fancy is a rare steak. Gret?
ISABELLA. I am of course a member of the / Church of England.*
GRET. Potatoes.
MARLENE. I haven't been to church for years. / I like Christmas carols.
ISABELLA. Good works matter more than church attendance.
MARLENE. Make that two steaks and a lot of potatoes. Rare. But I don't do good works either.

Here, then, we have an excellent example of scripted interruptions and simultaneous speech without a hint of anyone being impolite. These overlappings are perfectly normal – and in many ways even positive – elements of our everyday conversations. (Incidentally, the quotations in this book are presented in forms of layout which resemble the printed version of each script respectively. These forms do vary somewhat from one script to another, so the variations have been reflected in this text. Layout is examined in detail in Chapter 12.)

Helping out

Sometimes our interruptions are not made in order to agree or disagree, nor are they made to change the subject: they are to finish off someone else's speech. Some individuals are particularly prone to this, always trying to anticipate the ending of a sentence and leaping in just before the speaker has had time to finish. This can be an extremely irritating character trait; one which can of course be reproduced in scripted dialogue, often to humorous effect.

SAM: So, Mr Parks, we are going to have to block the –
PARKS: Drains.
SAM: Air vent. For the time being, while we reconstruct that part
    of the wall. Of course that doesn't mean you can't use the –
PARKS: The toilet.
SAM: The toilet. No, no you can use the toilet. It doesn't mean you
    can't use the fan –
PARKS: Fan, yes.
SAM: The fan, which works –
PARKS: When you pull the cord.
SAM: Which works quite efficiently. When you pull the cord, of
    course.
PARKS: Yes.

The character who wants to demonstrate that he or she has understood a speech by jumping in with the last word may not, in fact, understand very much at all. Similar humorous patterns may be set by an individual who habitually repeats the last word or phrase spoken. Couples who have lived together for a long time often slip into these sorts of habits of speech, either repeating the other's line (sometimes in an apparent show of subservience) or finishing the other's phrase (sometimes out of impatience or a desire to show control). There is a wonderful example of this, incidentally, in one of the pseudo-interviews with an old couple in the film *When Harry Met Sally* (writer, Nora Ephron).

Each of these aspects of dialogue, whether comic or not, is very far from formal, written speech: again, it is the interaction of characters which is important.

Verbal shorthand

Very often, when people speaking together know each other well, or when the speaker is aware that the listener has a particular knowledge of the topic under discussion, a type of verbal shorthand is used. The most obvious example is technical or professional jargon. At an airport information desk, one employee might ask a colleague if she knows the ETA of BD148; overhearing this, we might well know that ETA means Expected Arrival Time but would be much less likely to know that BD148 refers to a flight by British Midland (though we would probably assume that BD stood for some airline or other). Every workplace has its jargon and abbreviations, with limited and varied access for outsiders.

Scriptwriters have always delighted in playing with jargon, frequently satirising the pretentiousness of the language and pointing up the hollowness behind all the impressive-sounding words. An outstanding modern example is Caryl Churchill's *Serious Money*, set in the money markets of London; but Ben Jonson, too, was exploring how greed and emptiness can be wonderfully disguised by jargon-laden language in his play *The Alchemist*. In the following extract, Subtle and his assistant Face are in the process of fooling Mammon that through a marvellous knowledge of alchemy they are able to turn base metals into gold, though Mammon's friend Surly is not convinced:

SUBTLE: Look well to the register
    And let your heat, still, lessen by degrees,
    To the aludels.
FACE: Yes, sir.
SUBTLE: Did you look
    O' the bolt's head yet?
FACE: Which, on D, sir?
SUBTLE: Ay.
    What's the complexion?
FACE: Whitish.
SUBTLE: Infuse vinegar,
    To draw his volatile substance, and his tincture:
    And let the water in glass E be filtered,
    And put into the gripe's egg. Lute him well;
    And leave him closed in *balneo*.

FACE: I will, sir.
                                         [*Exit* FACE]
SURLY: What a brave language here is? Next to canting?

We do not know why the heat should be lessened, or what aludels are, or volatile substance, tincture, gripe's egg, luting or *balneo*. Neither would the vast majority of Jonson's original audience (though just as Caryl Churchill uses the authentic language of the City, so Jonson's terms are all taken from books on alchemy current at the time). We are not *meant* to understand jargon when it is presented in this way. Its purpose is to obscure meaning, and it does that very well! Of course, if there is no respite from such jargon in a whole script, then it might become tiresome; its use must not obstruct the audience's appreciation of characterisation, plot or other aspects of the production.

While we tend to reserve the term 'jargon' for words arising in a context of specialisation – at work, for example, or in sport – we often use types of verbal shorthand in everyday social contexts, too.

JACK: How much were they asking?
PHIL: Hundred and twenty thousand. Yeah well exactly.
JACK: And what did Judy say when –
PHIL: (*overlapping*) Well not at that price. And outside London –
JACK: She's always said –
PHIL: (*cutting in*) Exactly.
JACK: So are you going to keep looking?
PHIL: I suppose so.

This piece of conversation depends heavily on the shared knowledge and shared assumptions of the two speakers. They both know that Judy, the partner of Phil, doesn't really want to move out of London, and certainly not to somewhere more expensive. They only need to remind each other of these things, not to state them fully. Thus the 'Yeah well exactly,' which Phil adds to his first line is a response to the expression on Jack's face, as well as the shared knowledge of the expected reaction of Judy. As before, we see here a conversation which looks odd on the page but reflects language as we actually speak it.

Conversational ping-pong

Another way in which we may be tempted to turn the messiness of dialogue into something neater is by writing what might be termed 'conversational ping-pong'. In this form of fictional dialogue, every topic is clearly introduced (the serve). There is then a series of speeches, each a logical response to the previous one (the rally), and a new topic is only opened when the previous point has been finished with (the ball has gone out of play and there is a new serve). Conversational ping-pong is probably the most common form of poor dialogue produced by inexperienced scriptwriters.

So what is wrong with it? Simply, we very rarely talk in this way. Apart from anything else, in normal conversation more than one topic is frequently being dealt with at the same time (which in table tennis terms would mean two balls in play simultaneously!); any sort of predictable statement-and-response or question-and-answer pattern is broken up by all the factors already referred to, as well as a number of others. These include: dealing with misunderstandings which may arise, or not dealing with them and having the misunderstandings develop further; the occurrence of silences within conversation; a speaker going off at a tangent; or one speaker verbally responding not to the words of another but to some physical action. There is also the particular agenda and state of mind which each participant brings with him or her to the scene (more of this in the following chapter), which is likely to produce something even more complicated. In short, then, conversation is complex, and can rarely be reflected accurately by dialogue of the ping-pong variety.

It should also be pointed out that the pattern and style of any conversation is not just a product of the circumstances of that moment and that particular interaction, but is fundamentally affected by the background and individual character traits of each person present: dialogue is inextricably bound up with *characterisation*.

'Oh I say' and 'Ee by gum'

While all English speakers obviously speak the same language, every single one of us speaks it differently. Some characteristics of speech are specific to the individual, but others are the result of their place of origin, class, education and occupation. An individual's speech patterns will to some extent betray each of these elements, as well as some more personal attributes.

I began one play, *A Few Kind Words*, with the following speech:

> Allus bin willin' te mek an effort, all o' my life, when it wor needed. Which is more un can be said fer some folk. But yer got to. Yo mek your birr of an effort, tha meks tha'n an' that's ha yer goo on. Well it wor in mah day. Can't see uz 'ow it can change.

This, clearly, is not 'standard English', and it certainly demands to be spoken in an accent which is not 'received pronunciation'. The character speaking, Tommy, is a retired miner from Ilkeston, Derbyshire. I chose to write his part phonetically (though the BBC then unsuccessfully attempted to have me write it out again more conventionally) because I could foresee the difficulties that might arise for an actor if this character's speeches were presented with standard spelling:

> Always been willing to make an effort, all of my life, when it were needed...

No, the idea of having an actor try to turn this conventionally spelt language into that particular type of Derbyshire speech did not appeal to me. But it is not just a matter of the accent which marks out this language. There is also the vocabulary – 'tha meks tha'n' – which makes it Derbyshire speech of a certain sort. A little later Tommy refers to 'wock':

> ...thee'd no pride in wock, didn't know what real wock wor.

The dialect may already have given us a good idea of where Tommy comes from (as well as his class, education and possible occupation), but to listeners from that part of the Midlands this word 'wock' will sound a note of particular authenticity. A middle-aged person there at that time would say something like 'wairk'; a younger person might say 'werk' (with a longer vowel sound than the southern 'work'); but only an old person would persist with 'wock'. If one is going to write in dialect it has to be done properly!

There may be other occasions, when dealing with better-known dialects such as cockney, on which it is sufficient in terms of accent simply to put in a stage direction – for example, *In strong cockney accent* – and then to make sure that the vocabulary and phraseology are, in fact, cockney. Putting apostrophes for every "asn't' and 'wha" can in fact become tedious, though in the case of a very strong but less well-known dialect such as that of an old Ilkeston man I believe that the phonetic spelling was justified. (However, as the agent Julian Friedmann has recently pointed out to me, writing in dialect is not advisable for the writer who is not already established: initially it can be very off-putting for a scriptreader or prospective director.)

Whatever the difficulties of presentation on the page, then, there are clearly recognisable differences in speech arising from the background of each individual. Good written dialogue will certainly reflect these differences. What must be avoided, however (except in certain forms of comic writing, and even this is questionable), is the clichéd version of these differences, in which all upper-class characters pepper their speech with phrases such as 'Oh I say!', and anyone from north of Watford throws in a frequent 'Ee by gum!' for good measure. We must be aware of many more subtle mixes, such as the language used by the upper-class Lancastrian – neither Eton nor Coronation Street – or the speech of the well-educated middle-class woman who now lives on a working-class estate and has taken on some (but only some) of the speech characteristics of her adopted milieu. Perhaps she speaks in one way with her local friends and in another with certain members of her family. She may also speak rather differently when in male or in female company.

The gender gap

Many of us will be vaguely aware of differences in conversational style between men and women – a contrast which is probably stronger when the company is all-female or all-male. Of course, whichever gender we belong to, we cannot have had first-hand experience of a conversation between members exclusively of the opposite sex. We may suspect how such conversations might go, but we cannot be sure. Some academic research, however, helps us out here, and indeed quite a lot of research has been conducted on the differences between male and female types of speech[1], examining both style and content. Again, while stereotypes are to be

[1]These include SMITH, P. (1985) *Language, the Sexes and Society*, Oxford, Blackwell and TANNEN, D. (1991) *You Just Don't Understand*, London, Virago.

14

avoided (once more with the possible exception of their use in comedy), the consensus does seem to be that *in general* – and with many exceptions – there is a tendency for women to use language more as a tool of co-operation, less competitively than men. They may use it more to support each other and less as a means of control than men (women will tend to make more supportive interruptions than men); and more to genuinely 'connect' and less to impress with status than men (this is a paraphrase of a summary by Janet Holmes[2]). Of course, we will all know of many occasions when women have not conformed to these generalisations (starting with the first British female Prime Minister), and there are many women who appear consistently to have contradicted the research – but it is nevertheless useful to bear the generalisations in mind. If there were not some truth in them, after all, then surely all those comedies based upon the differences between men and women (particularly their styles of socialising) would cease to be so funny.

Social codes

Our conversations all take place within certain social conventions, and these have a major bearing upon how any piece of dialogue develops. These conventions are not entirely rigid – they vary according to class, background and situation – but there are certain generalisations which can be made. For example, in a group conversation in a pub, say, or at a dinner party, anecdotes will often be told in accordance with the unwritten rule that everyone should be given the opportunity to tell a story on a particular topic – holiday disasters, giving up smoking or whatever; we take it in turns. Keeping to this rule is normal; in a script, however, a point may be made by the *breaking* of such a rule. Perhaps a character is not given the chance to contribute an anecdote, or perhaps he or she can't think of anything to say. This is an example of dialogue conveying something not through the meaning of the words, but through its *form*.

Similarly, there are conventions which generally apply to the tone of any given conversation, or at least to parts of a conversation. If people are speaking in a jokey way, then a sudden change of tone to

[2]HOLMES, J. *The Role of Compliments in Female–Male Interaction* in MAYBIN and MERCER (Eds) (1996) *Using English, from Conversation to Canon*, London, Routledge.

the extremely serious might well be considered an irritation. The reverse – someone throwing a joke into an intense conversation about, say, death or politics – could be even more of a gaffe. Again, we have dialogue conveying something through the breaking of codes rather than through the meanings of words. In the successful American comedy series *Friends*, much of the humour associated with the character of Phoebe arises out of just such breaking of conventions – she never seems to quite understand the rules, so her odd interjections (trying to catch the tone but not quite succeeding) are both charming and funny. Similarly, in the television comedy series *The Royle Family*, Mam continually arrives in conversations from utterly unexpected directions; often she seems to come from a world of her own. In other scripts when a character breaks the conventions of conversation it might show arrogance, or rebelliousness: *how we handle codes through dialogue is central to characterisation.*

Culture clash

The differences in speech between Tommy in the extract above and the speech of the other characters in the play – particularly that of his own, well educated, daughter who has moved further south – reflect major social differences between them; indeed, these are a very important thematic element of the play. Yet the differences may be even greater than this when they are between characters who come from cultures as distinct as, for example, British Afro-Caribbean and British Asian, or between English speakers who were born and live in other countries, whether Singapore or New Zealand, the USA or India.

Each of these English-speaking cultures has its own vocabulary, grammar and style of speech. But it goes beyond this. For example, I have considerable experience of socialising with Latin Americans who speak English as a second language, and have learned that their rules of conversation are rather different from ours. When a new person is brought along to an English group, that person is introduced to the others but then is often left to sink or swim – he or she has to some extent to battle to make space in the conversation, to make a contribution. This is not seen as rude by the English: the new person is left to acclimatise to the group, and to pay them too much attention might even be seen as pressurising. To a Latin American, however, being treated in this way seems extremely impolite. Their social conventions (perhaps mirroring their wider cultural values, which also differ from ours) dictate that when a new person is introduced to a group, then much of the talk is directed to that person, and throughout the conversation strenuous efforts are made to ensure that the new person is included.

The scriptwriter must take note of these culture clashes in social conventions. Where a Latin American in an English group might feel insulted at being almost ignored (not understanding the codes), an English person in a Latin American group may gain an inflated idea of their own importance, not realising that the lavish attention they are receiving is a matter of social convention and does not necessarily reflect tremendous interest in this particular individual. This is one cultural clash in use of language of which I am aware, but there are certainly many more of which I am not aware between these two cultures, and of course there are countless more between all the other English-speaking cultures and sub-cultures.

As has already been noted, the development of any conversation is heavily dependent on social codes, and these we generally take for granted, as we tend to operate within groups from our own culture and sub-culture. *The danger for the scriptwriter is in making the assumption that people from other cultures or sub-cultures operate within the same rules.* We may notice the different accent, vocabulary, phraseology, and even the different ways of constructing sentences, but we must also make ourselves aware of the social codes which are in operation, if our scripted dialogue for characters from cultures and sub-cultures other than our own is to be convincing.

Our fingerprints of speech

We have looked at similarities in use of speech arising from similarities of background, yet if we think of the person who is most similar to ourselves – perhaps a relative or a best friend – and mentally try to re-create that person's style of speech, we will realise that despite everything we have in common with that person, their style of speech is still not the same as our own. This is the case despite our being of the same gender, and despite all the similarities that there may be in our background or occupation. One individual may have a tendency to speak in short, clipped phrases, another to ramble on in sentences which seem to go on for ever and where the sense occasionally gets lost. One may be

17

hesitant, almost stuttering and full of 'ums' and 'ers', another may always seem to speak with complete fluency. One may delight in being playful and humorous with language, another may only ever be literal. One may slip into elaborate story-telling at every opportunity, another may use language primarily as a tool with which to analyse every concept. One may use the ambiguity of language to distort ideas and manipulate people, another may only ever speak plainly and directly. One may continually interrupt, another may hardly ever do so. The list is almost endless.

And then there are the pet words and phrases. We all have preferences for particular words, sometimes to the point of exasperating those we are closest to. Our preferences are not always so obvious, however. I have realised that I tend to use the word 'just' a great deal, although not to the extent, I hope, that anyone else has ever noticed it. When it comes to pet phrases, some of us use the same phrase again and again even within one speech. 'As I say' and 'of course' continually occur, while 'you know', either alone or as part of a longer phrase, is equally popular. I was with a cab driver recently who finished almost every sentence with '...you know what I'm saying', and he still managed to work in 'Know what I mean' an impressive number of times as well! One friend of mine continually punctuates her speeches with, 'Well this is it', while another often repeats the less common 'It's like everything else...'. Many of these phrases are slipped in, along with 'ums' and 'ers' and repetitions, simply to give the speaker time to think, time to sort out what to say next. They may fulfil other functions as well, such as emphasising a point or making sure that the listener does agree.

The choice of precisely which words or phrases we habitually repeat – and how often we resort to them – may be partly mere habit, but it does say something about each of us. Many scriptwriters have latched on to this (and novelists too, incidentally, notably Dickens). In Michael Frayn's *Alphabetical Order*, for example, Leslie is continually saying 'Sorry', while John's verbal tic is 'as it were'. In Leslie's case, 'Sorry' keeps arising as she is aware that she is very often saying things which people do not want to hear, but which are generally correct nevertheless; at times the word expresses her embarrassment at her own directness, while at other times she does not seem sorry at all – rather, it seems to mean, 'Sorry, but I've just got to say it anyway and you've got to put up with it.' The one word encapsulates a major element of the character, including traits which are both irritating and admirable. John, on the other hand, endlessly uses variants of 'as it were' because he is never happy with his own way of expressing himself (he writes leader columns for a provincial newspaper, without conspicuous success); the phrase suggests, too, a more general uncertainty about his own opinions, and even about whom he feels himself to be. In the second act of the play the other characters increasingly use these phrases back at Leslie and John. There is an open acknowledgement of the use of these pet phrases, and with it a clearer acknowledgement also of exactly what makes these characters tick.

The words for the moment

We have seen that there are certain characteristics – such as class, education, area of origin and occupation – which we may have in common with others and which may affect our speech in fairly predictable ways; and that, in addition, there are other individual characteristics which will find their way into our speech patterns, differentiating one person's speech from that of the next. But how any of us uses language clearly has a further major ingredient – the circumstances of any particular occasion.

Each of us uses language in radically different ways depending upon the situation. The vocabulary, the phraseology, in fact every element of our speech varies enormously depending on the setting in which we speak; it is obvious that the same person will talk in quite different ways at a business meeting, at a football match, alone with a lover, at a child's birthday party or when drinking late at night with a close friend. We all have a range of 'registers' of speech (though we don't all have the same range). The writer of dialogue must differentiate the manner of speech of one character from that of another, but at the same time must not be afraid of using the whole range of registers employed by any one character. *It is too easy for a scriptwriter to pigeon-hole the speech of a character in an over-simplified way.* In the best scriptwriting, the major characters (and some of the others) will be given the opportunity to show the range of registers they use.

And then there is the small matter of *emotions*. When furious, for example, we may become positively incoherent, or start to use rhythm and repetition in a more marked way than at any other times:

I hate your Mum, I hate her house and I hate her ruddy dog!

19

Sometimes, of course, we make mistakes, we use the wrong register. A bad swear-word, one which you might use with your drinking partner, slips out in front of Grandma; or you find yourself talking to your lover in the sort of language you might use to an office junior – or to a boss. And these mistakes – the inappropriate word or the type of sentence which is out of place – also say something about the speaker at that moment, perhaps reflecting tensions or preoccupations, or revealing more general limitations or a lack of sensitivity on the part of an individual who does not even realise that he or she is using an inappropriate register.

So, the way in which we use language varies immensely from person to person, from situation to situation. Were we to know enough about ourselves and others, perhaps we would be able to say precisely why it is that each of our speeches takes the form that it does. But I am not suggesting that a scriptwriter should have to consciously analyse the psyche and every other aspect of each one of their fictional characters and, on the basis of that, supply them with appropriate language for each new occasion. *No, the writer should use their most effective tool: the ear.* The writer must make him- or herself specially aware of all the differences that exist between speech patterns, and should be constantly listening out for all the subtle variations between one person's speech and another's, between language used on one occasion and that used on another. Then the writer is in a position to introduce all these elements into the writing of dialogue.

Word-for-word transcription

All the examples given so far have been invented, either specifically for this book or for a script. Now we will look at some examples of people's actual speech, transcribed from tape recordings. First, here is Norma, a Scots woman talking about rationing and her childhood in general. Her parents ran a shop. Here, she is being formally interviewed:

NORMA: You only got so much each week, I don't remember what, but... We had bread units, and so much sugar each week. I remember the blue bags of sugar that we used to have to make up in the shop, and as a child I did this quite a lot. From a huge sack of sugar we'd make up the pound bags and fold them in a special way – do you remember that, no?

INTERVIEWER: (*overlapping*) No.

NORMA: And that was all during the war.

INTERVIEWER: Do you think those sorts of things had an effect on you?

pause

NORMA: I suppose they did inevitably, but I'm not conscious of that. I had a very innocent childhood, with no pressure whatsoever. You know, it was all just fun really. I suppose having parents with a shop – you know, I could go into the box and have a Mars Bar when I felt like it –

INTERVIEWER: (*interrupting*) Even during the war?

NORMA: Yes. That's wicked really, isn't it.

INTERVIEWER: (*simultaneous with above*) Whooa!

NORMA: I don't say it was necessarily a Mars Bar but... erm...

INTERVIEWER: (*speech simultaneous with above, but inaudible*)

NORMA: No, I don't remember it being difficult at all. It was fun. It must have been terrible to be a parent but I didn't feel any pressure at all.

The next example is of Dick, a North Bucks butcher. Again, it is a formal interview (though the interviewer is a different person). Like Norma, Dick comes from a shopkeeping family. Here he is talking about his father and grandfather.

DICK: One Saturday morning, our Sam wanted half a scone. You know what a scone is, don't you? And erm, they give him – give him a penny or something like that out the till, that was about that, so anyhow he come back. So he said, 'Dad,' he said, 'He wou'n't serve me with a scone.' His Dad says, 'What?' Says, 'Wou'n't serve me with one.' He says, 'Roight!' – straightaway, and he wrote him a letter (you understand, I'd barely know about this, but o' course we knew), course you see 'e'd – ooh my God! – didn't half carry on! 'Dear Mr so-and-so, I shall not want any more bread, as I'm starting making me own, and scones, which I'm going to break into. You got up in the world since you first come to Bradwell, when you used to ask me to bet your horse for you, 'cause you couldn't afford it didn't yer? Yours truly, Sam Tarry.' Yours truly, you know, not faithfully. Truly. (*laughs*) So that was that. Now then...

INTERVIEWER: So he started making his own bread. Did he keep to that –

DICK: Ooh, he, he used to, he make that – I'm telling you, well, it's the truth, used to make – he done it for about six months, and how long do you think it was interval between one batch of bread and the next? How long do you think it was? Well I won't ask yer. It was a month. Yeah. He used to get the yeast, he used to get the flour – home-made bread this is I'm talking – home-dried lard, which means the leaf out of a pig which had been rendered down and then allowed to set you see, and he'd put, he'd put, let's see what – some potatoes in it, boiled 'taters, and... a little bit of, now what is it now, powder summat... ooh by God boy you'd love some o' that. Phoo! Well, no comparis' – see it'd got some guts in it, hadn't it?

INTERVIEWER: But how did it manage to keep fresh for a month?

DICK: That was put in that pantry, on a board, and then put down, one on top o' the other, an' a big cloth over the top, do you follow me, in the pantry, in the shop. Well you see it was the salt content wa'n't it? He put a bit more salt in to allow for it, do you follow me. Ooh that was, look, fresh as a daisy. I should like some on it now. Oh yes. So that ain't a bad tale, is it?

Here, then, we have two sets of speeches. They have a number of factors in common. In neither case are they part of a normal conversation; they are more like monologues with occasional prompting. Since both people are being interviewed about their lives, they are both speaking in the same relatively formal situation. And finally, the speakers have in common an element of their backgrounds, in that they both come from families engaged in retailing. There, however, the similarities end. The differences between the two individuals are not restricted to the content of what each of them has to say; it is above all their style of speech which displays the dissimilarities.

Norma tends to speak in complete, grammatically correct sentences, though with the occasional hesitation and the odd unnecessary phrase thrown in. Transcribing this from the tape, I almost missed out the 'you know', partly because the phrase was uttered very fast – much faster than the rest of her speech – but also because my brain simply cancelled it out; from the continual practice that we have all had, my brain was telling me to focus as usual on the sense of what was being said, and in this respect the 'you know' was irrelevant. And this, of course, is what we do all the time: we dismiss the little added phrases, very often not even realising that they are there. *But they are there, and the writer must be aware of them.*

Dick's style of speech is very different indeed. He is much more willing to restart sentences, to use filler words and phrases and to throw in the odd pet phrase as well. For example, 'Do you follow me?' occurs many times later in the interview. He adds to his thoughts as he goes along, throwing in new phrases and ideas as they occur to him in the middle of saying something else, and is less concerned than Norma with speaking in complete sentences. He will often leave words out, too:

His Dad says, 'What?' Says, 'Woun't serve me with one.'

Here he leaves out 'Sam' before 'Says', and also the 'He' before 'Woun't': meaning is more important than grammar, and Dick is quite happy to leave out the subject of the sentence rather than slow the story up with extra words. His concern is to dramatise, to bring his thoughts to life, so he happily mixes the present tense with the past tense to tell his story – which is very much a story – as the present tense helps to make the events of the past feel so much more immediate:

He says, 'Roight!' – straight away, and he wrote him a letter...

At one point he tells the interviewer:

Well, no comparis' – see it'd got some guts in it, hadn't it?

Here he can't be bothered to finish the word 'comparison', as he interrupts himself with a stronger way of expressing what he wants to say. This is language where the thoughts seem to come out virtually *unprocessed*, and it is language which the scriptwriter would do well to try to imitate.

Dick's use of English is much further from 'standard' than is Norma's. Dick will say 'something like that out the till' rather than 'out of the till', or 'I should like some on it' rather than 'I should like some of it', and he will use words like 'summat'. (Note that he comes from Buckinghamshire – careful listening reminds us that use of this and many other such words and phrases, such as 'My duck', is not restricted to northerners.) Norma's vocabulary, at least in this extract, is entirely standard, and despite her Scots origins even her accent is closer to 'received pronunciation' than is that of Home Counties-born Dick. Thus in transcribing I felt no need to write any of Norma's words phonetically, while for the other transcription I couldn't resist writing 'Roight' (and I could well have put 'clorth' for 'cloth' as well). This says more about their relative class backgrounds than about their geographical origins – both their parents may have been retailers, but they were not from the same strata of society.

Judging from the page, one might be tempted to conclude that Dick is not particularly intelligent, but such a conclusion would be entirely wrong. His is not an educated style of speech, but neither is he in fact confused in what he is saying; he is certainly intelligent. The problem is that we are used to written speech which has been tidied up; very often editors tidy up the language even in books compiled from taped reminiscence! Similarly, for many years script-writers would create fictional characters who spoke in ways that were similar to Dick's speech only when they wanted to portray simpletons. More recently that has changed, as writers have more accurately reflected how we speak and the ways in which our speech shows what we are.

As pointed out earlier, of course a writer does not have to have made a detailed analysis of a character before setting out to script the speeches of that character (though actually, many writers do find just such an exercise useful in really pinning down exactly who – or what – that character is). Rather, in some cases a character's speech might be based upon a particular individual known to the writer, or a careful mix of a number of individuals known to the writer, so very little actual analysis of the use of language by the character might be necessary. However, for this straightfor-ward, non-analytical approach to succeed, the writer must have developed the habit of noticing, studying and remembering various speech patterns, so that they can then be called up at will as the need arises.

Habitual styles of speech – even those of characters from fairly similar backgrounds – differ as greatly as do Norma's from Dick's. We must never tire of listening for the variations.

2. The Characters' Agendas

What we want

In Chapter 1 we looked at many of the aspects of how normal conversation works. In this chapter we will look at one further aspect – the *agendas* which each one of us brings to each conversation, and we will examine the effects that these agendas have.

Whenever we begin speaking with someone, we have a personal agenda. This is some sort of idea of what we want from the conversation. We might want to communicate something specific, or to find out something. There might be only one item on the agenda and it may be relatively trivial, such as, 'I must tell Shirley about the special offer at the supermarket.' In this case the agenda (or at least the initial agenda, since an agenda may alter as the conversation evolves) can be dealt with very easily: 'Oh Shirley, did you know they're doing salmon at half price in Sainsbury's?' – and that's it. On another occasion an agenda might consist of a number of items, none of which is trivial. For example, a man meeting his partner after a long separation might have an agenda consisting of the following, not necessarily in this order: (a) making it clear to her how much he has missed her; (b) telling her how well he has used the time while she has been away; (c) the need to sort out major financial problems. Immediately, it may be seen that there are different types of items on this agenda: (a) is concerned with emotions; (b) is also at least partly about emotions, as he is trying to make her feel more positively towards him by impressing her with his use of time; (c) is mainly dealing with practicalities, but this item too has a bearing on the relationship (how many couples have broken up over conflicts involving money?).

It is becoming apparent already that none of these agenda items is watertight – they tend to seep into each other, so that even while you are dealing with one item you find yourself dealing with another. Thus, while this man is telling his partner how much he has achieved – decorating the house, say – while she has been away, he may also take the opportunity of saying how he was thinking of her all the time as he was doing it, and how he was looking forward to seeing her face when she saw it. Or – a slightly less harmonious combination – he might at the same time introduce the matter of how much all the redecoration has cost, priming her for a later, fuller discussion of finances.

The agenda and the script

So, how does all this relate to effective scriptwriting? The first point to make is that most writers are aware that characters have some sort of agenda for each conversation (though they may confuse it with their own agenda, which we will discuss later); but the ineffective scriptwriter will over-compartmentalise, so that a conversation clearly deals with one topic, then another. This is a close relative of conversational ping-pong, discussed in Chapter 1. Sometimes, of course, that is what happens in life, but very often conversation is not like that – we are opportunistic, slipping from one item of our agenda to another as the opportunity arises.

Sometimes we know exactly what we want to talk about in a conversation – we have a *conscious agenda*. This is obviously the case in, for example, business meetings (though neither side's agenda may correspond entirely to the agreed written agenda – each side in a business meeting may well also have a conscious 'hidden agenda'). On other occasions, we may have little or no idea of what we want to say or what we want to achieve; thus when out for a drink with a friend we might not be conscious of any agenda beyond 'having a good night out'. But none of this acknowledges the crucial role of the semi-conscious and unconscious agenda. Let us revert to our original example, 'I must tell Shirley about the special offer at the supermarket.' This item may be dealt with in many different ways, depending upon what other semi-conscious or unconscious agendas also exist:

Oh, Shirley, I'm actually really quite fed up with salmon – it used to be special, didn't it? – but anyway I thought you might like to know, there's this special offer at Sainsbury's – they're doing it at half price.

Here the speaker also has another item on her agenda – wanting to impress with her superiority of taste (this may well be a permanent agenda item for this individual!). Or the topic might be dealt with quite differently:

> Shirl, it's not extravagant, it's really not, 'cause at that price it's no more than a can of tuna – but they're doing salmon at half price down Sainsbury's. Did you know?

Here again, the speaker is not merely imparting information, as another agenda item is her desire to make clear to her friend that she is not being extravagant.

Very often, then, there is a slant on one agenda item – the slant being, in fact, another agenda item. Rather than being presented baldly, a topic is dealt with in such a way as to serve some other purpose at the same time; to deal with some other agenda. At its strongest this can have the effect of giving a piece of dialogue what is sometimes called an 'edge', a feeling of not entirely explained tension. This can arise when a character is openly presenting an opinion on one item agenda, but at the same time is indirectly presenting a contradictory opinion on another, connected, agenda item. So there might be, say, a conversation in which one character is praising another for all that she has achieved as a business woman, but at the same time cannot conceal feeling bitterly angry and jealous of her for that very same achievement. The conflict between these two agenda items produces an edge.

Who has control?

So far we have looked only at the agenda of any one individual in conversation. In fact, of course, there is always more than one agenda in dialogue, as there is always more than one individual taking part. Sometimes we will politely take it in turns to go through our agendas. After talking about ourselves, we might then ask, 'And how about you?', thus passing the initiative over to the other person. On other occasions exactly the same happens but with a less obvious cue: one character simply leaves the space for the other one to take over. Very often, however, the movement from one individual's agenda item to another's is nowhere near as clear as this. Examine the following two examples:

Example 1

PETE: Are you going to the disco tonight?
ALAN: Dunno.
PETE: Julie'll be there.
ALAN: Julie?
PETE: You know, the bubbly one, with the legs.
ALAN: Oh Julie.
PETE: Yeah, Julie.
 slight pause
ALAN: I got beaten at snooker again last night.
PETE: Yeah?
ALAN: It's that Brian – he cheats.
PETE: Oh.
 You can't cheat at snooker. How can you cheat at snooker?
ALAN: It's the adding up.
PETE: How do you mean?
ALAN: Well, he can do it and I can't.
PETE: Ah.

Example 2

PETE: Are you going to the disco?
ALAN: Dunno.
 I got beaten at snooker again last night.
PETE: Yeah?
ALAN: It's that Brian. He cheats.
PETE: Oh.
 Julie'll be there. At the disco.
ALAN: Julie?
PETE: You know, the bubbly one, with the legs.
ALAN: Oh Julie.
PETE: Yeah, Julie.
 slight pause
PETE: You can't cheat at snooker. How can you cheat at snooker?
ALAN: It's the adding up.
PETE: How do you mean?
ALAN: Well, he can do it and I can't.
PETE: Ah.

The two examples are obviously extremely similar: each character speaks almost identical lines in each example, and in each they also have their own clear agendas – Pete wants to tell Alan about the disco and see how he reacts to the mention of Julie, while Alan wants to moan about Brian and the snooker. The difference, technically, is simply the order of the speeches, but that difference also says something about how these two characters relate to each other. In the first example, one topic is dealt with and finished with (at least for the moment) before we move on to the other character's agenda. In the second example the two topics are dealt with at the same time. The characters certainly listen to each other and are not rude – they reply to each other – but each of them turns the conversation back to their own agenda. At the end of the second example, though, there is a swap, as it is Pete who brings the conversation back to the snooker; he has adopted Alan's agenda.

Both the above examples are fairly successful pieces of dialogue. What the scriptwriter needs to recognise is that depending on the particular characters and situation, both types occur in real life and should be represented in scripts. A complete script written entirely in the form of Example 1 might seem too consistently direct and blunt, while one written entirely in the form of Example 2 could well become tiresome.

Of course, a scriptwriter may not always sit down before every scene and ask, 'What does each character want in this scene?' before writing it (though it is not at all a bad idea to do so), but he or she does have to be acutely aware of the particular histories and tensions that already exist between characters – their on-going, semi-conscious agendas – as well as any characters' concerns that are specific to that scene. In this way, every piece of dialogue is informed with the characters' attitudes, with the possibility of 'edge'. Any failure to do this will result in dialogue which is bland and, ultimately, uninteresting.

Pinter takes to extremes the conflict over control of the agendas, while sometimes Stoppard has his characters hardly attend to each other's lines at all, so intent are they on following through what is important to themselves. The following extract is from Stoppard's *Albert's Bridge*:

MOTHER: Ring for Kate, would you, Albert?
ALBERT: (*going*) Yes, mother.
MOTHER: That reminds me.
FATHER: You'll start where I started. On the shop floor.

29

ALBERT: (*approach*) Well, actually, Father –

MOTHER: I don't want to sound Victorian, but one can't just turn a blind eye.

ALBERT: What?

FATHER: Yes, I never went in for books and philosophy and look at me now.

MOTHER: I suppose that's the penance one pays for having servants nowadays.

ALBERT: What?

FATHER: I started Metal Alloys and Allied Metals – built it up from a biscuit tin furnace in the back garden, small melting jobs in the cycle-repair shop.

MOTHER: I've suspected it for some time and now one can't ignore it. Even with her corset.

ALBERT: Who?

FATHER: You can come in on Monday and I'll hand you over to the plant foreman.

ALBERT: I've already got a job. Actually.

FATHER: You haven't got a job till I give you one.

ALBERT: I'm going to paint Clufton Bay Bridge, starting Monday.

MOTHER: What colour?

ALBERT: Silver.

FATHER: Just a minute –

KATE: (*off*) You rang, madam?

More will be said about this passage later, but here we need only note how little these characters listen to each other, and thus how they relate – or fail to relate – to each other. Father is concerned only to lay down the law about his son's job, and Mother wishes only to voice her concerns about the likely pregnancy of Kate, the maid. Albert – who is in fact affected by both these topics far more directly than either of his parents – is put in the position of having to respond and trying to make sense of it all, and it is his lack of control of the agendas that adds much to the humour of the scene, particularly as we already know both that he does already have a job, and that he is almost certainly responsible for Kate's condition. An added touch of humour is provided by Mother's 'What colour?': she has listened to Father's statement but has not attended to the tone – the humour arises out of the triviality of the question set against the seriousness of the topic.

30

'What do you *want* from that line?'

I was once present at a play rehearsal at which an excellent director was leading a detailed examination of the script. Before every line the director would turn to the relevant actor and ask, 'What do you want to achieve with this?', meaning, 'What do you think the character you are playing *wants to get* as a result of saying (or sometimes doing) this?' Sometimes the answers were easy, but on other occasions the actors found it very difficult to say what the character was trying to achieve – what his or her agenda was – beyond, say, the straightforward requesting or sharing of information, or expression of emotion. Yet our motivations for saying things are often very complex, and there is a compelling theory which states that we want to 'get something out of' everything we say – that there are no utterances that are simply themselves[3]. What we can be certain of is that during any conversation, each of us has a whole set of agenda items, some of them specific to that conversation and others of them semi-permanent, such as perhaps wishing to raise our own status relative to that of others. It is the simultaneous operation of a number of these agenda items which lends much of the fascination to dialogue.

Before moving on we should pay a little further attention to the issue of status. In his fascinating book *Impro, Improvisation and the Theatre*[4], Keith Johnstone explores the proposition that much of our speech – and action – attempts to raise our status relative to that of those around us. Very often this is not done in an obvious way – 'My son's going to Oxford. I should think yours will get on well at the Tech.' – but rather it is subtle, with people trying to establish their status as being just slightly above that of their neighbour. This way not only is vulgarity avoided, but it is also easy to deny that any attempt at raising status is taking place. Frequently, indeed, people are competing for status while attempting to appear supportive and friendly:

JOHN: It was terrible. I thought I was going to get stuck under the
    boat!
ANDY: That's really scary, isn't it, when you capsize.

[3]MAX STAFFORD CLARKE presents this approach very persuasively in *Letters to George: the account of a rehearsal*, London, Nick Hern.
[4]KEITH JOHNSTONE (1979) *Impro, Improvisation and the Theatre*, London, Methuen.

31

JOHN: It certainly is!

TIM: At least the first time.

ANDY: I remember once when we went over I actually was stuck under the boat – only for a while of course. And it was in October.

TIM: The water must have been freezing.

ANDY: It was.

TIM: I was hit by the boom once. I was actually unconscious. It's just incredibly lucky that I wasn't sailing single-handed or –

ANDY: (*laughing*) But it's a bit stupid letting yourself get hit by the boom, isn't it?

Here we have three men, all apparently being friendly and support-ive of each other, yet in fact competing with each other for status. John begins by raising his status (a little) by being involved in an interesting incident, and one that felt dangerous. Andy begins by sympathising, while Tim greatly reduces John's status by stating that yes, capsizing can be 'scary', but at the same time making it clear that the fear lessens progressively each time one capsizes – thus making it clear that for him, capsizing is really quite routine. Andy then recounts a more seriously dangerous capsizing than John's, thus raising his own status at John's expense. John now drops out of the race – and, for the moment, the dialogue – as he realises he cannot compete with these two. Tim then sympathises with Andy – re-establishing his credentials of friendship – before recounting his own experience which was even more dangerous. At this point, though, rather than accept defeat, Andy laughs – the laugh is intended to emphasise that he is not seriously criticising, thus disguising the status-lowering intention – undermining the basis of Tim's claim to high status: his experience may have been more dangerous but he had also been more stupid, so perhaps this stupidity cancels out altogether any status claim from this incident. The terms of status acquisition in this particular piece of dialogue are being questioned.

There may be some characters who hardly indulge in raising or lowering status, while others seem interested in doing little else, but there must be few people indeed who are never involved in these games. The scriptwriter must be aware of these manoeuvres used to raise or lower status. It hardly needs to be said that the speakers themselves are often either unconscious or only semi-conscious of exactly what is going on, but the scriptwriter needs to be as conscious as possible. As with other aspects of scripting, though, the writer needs to develop the habit of taking note of exactly how these manoeuvres take place in everyday life; they will then be incorporated into scripting almost effortlessly.

Status changes

Let us continue the above dialogue a little further. It could go like this:

TIM: (*laughing*) I had a hell of a bump on my head, I can tell you!
  slight pause
JOHN: You know that money I inherited.
ANDY: Nnn.
JOHN: Well I'm thinking of buying a yacht.
ANDY: A yacht?!
JOHN: Only a small one. About thirty foot.
ANDY: Doesn't sound that small to me. But... would you know how to sail it?
JOHN: There are training courses. I'd go on one of those. I don't suppose it's all that difficult, but you ought to learn properly, if you're going to be serious about it, don't you think?
ANDY: Well yes, I suppose you're right.
TIM: So are you completely set on this?
JOHN: Not totally.
TIM: Only – don't get me wrong – I mean I've been on yachts a number of times, and it's great, but it's not quite as *exciting* as dinghy sailing. It's a bit more sedate really. Well it's bound to be isn't it. You're not leaping around the whole –
JOHN: (*overlapping*) But I don't think I *want* to be leaping around the whole time.
TIM: Fine. Well, maybe... maybe a yacht's the thing for you then.

In this passage we have dialogue which produces a clear *change* in status. This is important. Status is not static, but is always relative to the others present, and fluctuates depending upon what is being said or done. Thus a junior college lecturer might generally adopt high status relative to his or her students, but low status relative to many colleagues; he or she might be high status when taking a nephew to a classical concert, but low status when dragged along by that same nephew to a football match (the lecturer knowing nothing about football). An audience recognises and enjoys observing status changes, and status reverses are even better.

So, what exactly happens in the passage above? First, following on from the previous passage, Tim joins in the laughter, but his first line, 'I had a hell of a bump on my head, I can tell you!' only hints at accepting the stupidity of which he has been accused. At the same time it emphasises again – though now in the jokey manner established by Andy – the seriousness of the incident: he is not going to have his status reduced very far.

Then John, who has been silent for a little while, brings up the subject of his proposed purchase of a yacht. This, of course, raises his status immediately, a yacht being much more impressive than a dinghy. Andy accepts this raising of John's status (and thus the relative lowering of his own), although he does question whether John would actually know how to sail it. Even this, though, John turns to his owns advantage, emphasising his own professional approach, which further raises his status. Tim, however, does not surrender his status so easily. He attempts to lower the status of yachting itself, and thus that of John, by questioning how exciting it can possibly be. John refuses to relinquish his new high status: by stating that he does not wish to be 'leaping around the whole time' he implies that dinghy sailing is an inferior activity. Tim pretends to accept this, but the tone of his final speech at the same time makes clear that while yachting might be the thing for John, it certainly would not be for him. A sort of status stalemate has been reached.

Of course, it could well be said that I am putting forward a very cynical view of the world – or at least of an important element of how dialogue functions. Certainly I am aware that some people refuse to play status games, at least consciously, unless they feel they are absolutely forced into it; and there are some who actually view any attempt to raise status – however subtle – as something negative about that individual (if they were thinking in status terms, then, trying to raise status would automatically result in a lowering of it). Nevertheless, if we observe closely what people are trying to achieve moment-to-moment in dialogue, for very many people status is close to the heart of it.

Lowering status

Certainly, different individuals have different attitudes towards status, some ruthlessly using it, others doing so much less aggressively. Sometimes we learn, too, that attempting to use status – or even unintentionally allowing it to come into a conversation – can have negative results. For example, a nuclear physicist may have a friendly, chatty relationship with his or her hairdresser – until the hairdresser finds out what the customer does for a living. Now the hairdresser feels ignorant and inhibited in such company, and clams up completely for fear of looking foolish. The nuclear physicist changes to another hairdresser, and this time refuses to be drawn on his or her profession, or perhaps pretends to be something different altogether – a taxi driver or whatever. The relationship with this new hairdresser is allowed to continue to be friendly and chatty, though there is now a different awkwardness – of the nuclear physicist always having to be careful in order not to be discovered.

Or let us take another example. A wealthy female psychiatrist has a daughter who attends a state school, where most of the children come from a very different background. The girl is having some problems, so the psychiatrist, her mother, visits the (male) Headteacher:

HEADTEACHER: (*opening the door*) Come in, Mrs Waring.
WARING: (*coming in*) Thank you. Actually, it's...
HEADTEACHER: I'm sorry?
WARING: No, nothing.
HEADTEACHER: Well, sorry to have kept you waiting so long.
WARING: It's all right – thanks for taking the time to see me.
HEADTEACHER: A pleasure. Now, what can I do for you?
WARING: Well it's about my daughter, obviously...
HEADTEACHER: Yes.
SECRETARY: (*poking her head round the door*) I'm sorry to bother you, but the Mercedes outside – is it yours?
WARING: Well I –
SECRETARY: Only it's blocking the school coach.
WARING: (to HEADTEACHER) It's a bit of a rust bucket actually.
SECRETARY: It's –
WARING: Yes, right. Won't be a moment.

At the start of this exchange, Waring almost corrects the Headteacher by telling him that she is in fact Doctor rather than Mrs Waring, but she stops herself. Then, 'Thanks for taking the time to see me' very slightly lowers her own status. She might, after all, have adopted a very different tone in response to having been kept waiting for some time. When they are interrupted by the Secretary mentioning the Mercedes, Waring then tries to lower the status of that too, but this time she is unsuccessful, succeeding only in saying something rather silly and unconvincing – 'It's a bit of a rust bucket actually.' But why might Waring wish to lower her own status in this way? The most likely answer is that she has experienced in the past some negative reactions to the high status that accompanies both her occupation and her wealth. Some people feel threatened by high status, particularly high status in a woman, and this can make them try very hard to compete (which can at best be embarrassing), or can lead them to feel directly antagonistic – 'She needn't think that by wandering in here with her Mercedes and her swanky job she'll be treated any differently from anyone else!' Waring wants the co-operation of the Headteacher, and as far as possible she doesn't want status to get in the way of that, so she chooses to reduce her own status and, in the process, to raise that of the Headteacher.

As we have discussed in this chapter, status can change within scenes. There can also be long-term status changes, ones which can take place over the course of a whole script. These may be of beggar-to-Prince or Prince-to-beggar proportions. It is not only fairy-tales which delight in these status changes. There is that wonderful moment in the film *Pretty Woman* (writer, J. F. Lawton) where the woman who previously had looked rather like a prostitute (because she is one) returns to the decidedly up-market clothes store where just the day before she had been refused service by two shop assistants who had clearly considered it below their status and the status of their shop to have this woman even on the premises. This time, she is dressed with real elegance (and at obvious real expense), and the same two assistants – not recognising her – are about to be positively fawning when she tells them of the massive scale of their mistake the previous day – and makes it clear that she will not be buying anything from them. They are duly appalled and we are duly delighted.

Or we might turn to the film *Goodfellas* (writers, Martin Scorsese and Nicholas Pileggi from Pileggi's novel), in which we witness the gradual rise in status of Henry – and the corresponding change in the language by which he is addressed. These are status alterations on a big scale, but very often dialogue charts status changes across the length of a script in the more subtle ways of the earlier examples.

Letting the action run

The question posed by that director – 'What do you [the character] *want* from that line?' – is a good one for a scriptwriter, too, to pose at frequent points in the process of drafting and re-drafting a script. 'What was her agenda item here? Might she stay on that point a little longer? Might her resentment from the earlier incident show through here?' This sort of detailed questioning of motivation for every line is invaluable. I would suggest, however, that it should take place not at the moment of first draft but later. For that first draft the writer must, in a sense, allow each scene to 'write itself'. Scriptwriters will often say things like, 'the characters just ran away with the story,' 'the characters took over,' or 'I didn't mean it to go in that direction but I found it did anyway.' This is what I mean by letting the dialogue in each scene – *each* scene, and thus ultimately the whole script – 'write itself'. The phrase is of course absurd, as the writer does the writing, not the characters; but for a scene to really work it should be as if – *at the very moment of writing the first draft* – the characters are speaking those lines at that instant. You, the writer – hearing the characters' inflections in your head, letting their lines spark off each other spontaneously, allowing the dialogue to take on a life of its own – are merely transcribing what you hear. In order for this to be successful, however, the writer must first, before starting upon the scene, think very carefully about its particular setting and also about each of the characters – their motivations, their backgrounds, their relationships to each other and their particular agendas. Then, when you are ready, you start, and it is as if they were there waiting for you: you switch them on and then just try to keep up with them as they subtly hint at this agenda item and that – as they try to *get what they want* from each line of the conversation.

Remember, though, that your characters may surprise you: through the interaction of their personalities, motivations and agendas they may suddenly take your dialogue into quite uncharted territory, which you would never have predicted and which you certainly never planned. This might profoundly disturb even the basis of your plot. This is a good sign! If the dialogue is strong, if the characters are truly interacting through it (or truly 'quasi-interacting' as in the Stoppard above) then the conflict – or the fusion – will always be leading to new territory. The scriptwriter must learn to embrace this, to welcome the apparently dangerous, not to inhibit it: the writer must run with it, allowing the dialogue to move in whatever direction the interaction takes it. Only by allowing this to happen does the writer allow real vitality into a scene.

After all, a scene can always be (and almost always should be) redrafted. It is then, in cool, analytical mode, that the writer has to make decisions on whether or not to follow up some of the new leads which have emerged in the scene which he or she has just written. Quite apart from making any adjustments to plans for the rest of the script, the writer may at this point add some lines, alter others, change the position of yet others and – most important of all – delete those which are not paying their way. But if in the first instance the writer has not allowed the dialogue to 'write itself' – has not allowed a genuine element of spontaneity – then it will probably never really rise above the pedestrian, and as a result may well fail to hold the audience.

Constant reworking

It is often assumed that revising a script is something that happens when a first draft has been completed. That is, of course, true, but it is not the whole truth. The scriptwriter must also rework scenes while the script is still in the process of being written, rereading and revising the last scenes that he or she has written before continuing with the new ones. Of course, a writer who simply makes a scene-by-scene plan for a script and sticks to it rigidly will have no need to make such running revisions, but such a procedure is unlikely to result in work of real merit, and certainly does not accommodate the somewhat unpredictable outcome of setting up a scene and then letting it 'write itself'. However thoroughly thought-out in advance a plan may be, the 'I've-written-my-plan-and-I'm-sticking-to-it' approach will have a tendency to lead to static characterisation, unsubtle relationships, a certain blandness and, as a result, ultimately rather dull dialogue. This is because the writer is scared to give the characters any freedom: they are being strait-jacketed by the *writer's* agenda – quite a different animal from the agendas of any of the characters. At the outset of writing a scene, the scriptwriter should of course have certain aims in mind in terms of development of relationships, character, plot, etc; in the setting of the scene and decisions as to when characters enter or leave, the scene should be set up to allow these aims to be accomplished. However, if these considerations are seen as paramount, so that the first priority for the dialogue is that it should be engineered for these purposes, then the result is inevitably a lack of life, a woodenness. The other approach, relying first upon a clear understanding of character, motivation, specific situation and individual agendas, then allowing the dialogue – and through it all the other aspects – to *develop* (and letting the characters' agendas change throughout the scene, too), calls for a certain bravery, an embracing of the difficult, the contradictory, the subtle. It also requires constant reworking in order that the writer may keep up with his or her own creativity. The rewards, though, are well worth the effort.

We should perhaps note here that, while each character has an agenda, those agendas do not need to be explicitly stated anywhere in the dialogue. Take, for example, the following exchange:

JANICE: Ah... I know what it is. It's because you resent Dad – that's what this is all really about, isn't it?

NOEL: Did I say that?

JANICE: You didn't need to. You resent Dad living here, and you can't keep yourself from showing it.

This piece of dialogue may function perfectly well, probably working best if the audience is to learn from it that *Janice has suddenly realised* that Noel resents her father living in the house. If, on the other hand, these speeches are included merely to inform the otherwise ignorant audience that Noel's words and actions have been affected by his resentment of the presence of Janice's father, then these speeches are probably at best superfluous, at worst damaging to the script. The audience should be left to work out characters' agendas for themselves, rather than being spoon-fed with them (in fact, spoon-feeding an audience in any way is to be avoided). An audience enjoys the experience of working things out – a process that draws them further into the production – and may well feel patronised by being told what they would rather have deduced. Furthermore, having agenda items spelt out in the dialogue can produce a laziness in the writing: why go to all the trouble of subtly showing a motivation when you can simply get a character to tell us about it? In this sense, as in many others, showing is greatly preferable to telling. (The writer can of course 'show' all sorts of things through dialogue as well as action, without anyone 'telling' anyone what is going on at all.)

More is said on the reworking of dialogue in Chapter 13, but here just one point should be noted. Almost all writers these days work on word processors or computers; these make altering text very much easier than it was in the days of the typewriter. When scriptwriters come to redrafting the whole text, producing a second and then a third draft, they are usually very careful to keep a copy of each draft on a separate file. However, in the actual process of writing that first draft (and any completely new material in later drafts), the writer should take just as much care to keep separate files of first versions of individual scenes – those first versions which have been written by allowing the dialogue to 'write itself', before any initial alterations. As I know to my cost, it really is infuriating to find that – having changed your mind and then changed it back again about how a section of dialogue should develop – you kept no copy of that very first version and now you are having to try to reconstruct it from memory. Recreating spontaneity is not easy: it is, after all, a contradiction in terms.

3. Naturalistic Dialogue

Beginnings and endings

Let us assume for one more chapter that the dialogue a scriptwriter is trying to get down on to the page is a replica of language just as we speak it. It has already been noted that very often this is not in fact what the writer is trying to do, but it is nevertheless a very useful starting point for us.

First, we have to deal with a little confusion over the correct term to use for this type of dialogue – the attempt to reproduce language as we speak it. There are two terms used for this, 'realism' and 'naturalism', both of which carry with them overtones from literary or artistic history; 'realism' also brings with it both 'realist' and 'realistic', which tends only to confuse matters further. A member of an audience might, for example, describe a piece of dialogue as 'not realistic', but this could mean either that the person did not think the dialogue was convincing – it was not convincingly realistic – or that they did not think the dialogue was written in the style of realism, i.e. that it was not attempting to imitate language as it is normally spoken. Because of this, I find 'naturalism' the less confusing term – despite the fact that it is also used to identify a certain (mainly French) school of nineteenth century writing – and so it is the one I prefer when referring to this style of dialogue.

We have already noted in the first chapter many elements of naturalistic dialogue. These include a consciousness of the class, gender, geographical origins and upbringing of each speaker as well as the particular register employed for the specific setting. We looked at how each individual will tend towards a particular phraseology, use of certain vocabulary and even, in some cases, distinctive sentence construction. Then, naturalistic dialogue has to conform to the general messiness of spoken language – the unfinished or ungrammatical sentences, hesitations, repetitions, interruptions, simultaneous

41

speeches and verbal shorthands, much of it resulting from interaction between individuals. In Chapter 2 we went on to look in detail at how dialogue is fundamentally affected by the agendas – conscious, semi-conscious and unconscious – of each character. So, is there nothing more to be said? When the scriptwriter feels confident about the use of all of this, does he or she then simply set about reproducing it, as a 'slice of life'? No, it is not quite so simple.

The first point to make concerns the beginning and ending of any piece of dialogue. In real life, a conversation might begin as follows:

> *Ringing of door bell.*
> PAULINE: Coming!
> *PAULINE opens the front door.*
> PAULINE: Oh! Jane, how're you doing?
> JANE: I'm fine.
> PAULINE: Well come in, come in.
> JANE: You're not busy are you? 'Cause I can always...
> PAULINE: (*overlapping with above*) No, I just I wasn't expecting – No, no, course I'm not.
> JANE: Only I wouldn't want to –
> PAULINE: No, it's fine. Like a cup of tea?
> JANE: ... Yeah, I'd love one.
> PAULINE: (*going into kitchen*) Lucky I've just brewed one.
>   *slight pause*
> JANE: It's lovely weather out there.
> PAULINE: (*from kitchen*) Yeah, it looks it.
> JANE: Warm, but there's still that chilly wind.
> PAULINE: (*from kitchen*)Yeah.
>   *slight pause*
> PAULINE: (*coming back from kitchen, carrying mugs of tea*) You don't take sugar, do you?
> JANE: Just one, please.
> PAULINE: Oh, right, just a mo.
> PAULINE *goes back into kitchen.*
> PAULINE: (*from kitchen*) So, how are you?
> JANE: Oh, I'm fine.
> PAULINE: (*coming back in*) The kids?
> JANE: Fine.
>   Do you mind if I use your loo?

PAULINE: You know where it is.

JANE: Yeah.

> *JANE goes upstairs. PAULINE sits and drinks her tea for a couple of minutes, browsing through a magazine.*
>
> *JANE comes back downstairs.*

JANE: Well, you're looking well.

PAULINE: Thanks.

> Well, we haven't seen each other for a long time, not since the wedding.

JANE: Yes. The wedding.

There are a number of points to be made about this piece of dialogue. The first is that it is utterly tedious. Yet it corresponds pretty accurately to dialogue as we speak it. Why, then, does it fail as part of a script? The answer is that the writer has joined the dialogue – joined the scene – too early. Of course, this is just the sort of opening to a conversation which might take place, before moving on to (perhaps!) more interesting matters; but there is no obligation upon the writer to start here – he or she can join a scene wherever seems appropriate, certainly missing any such tedious openings. The same applies to endings: many conversations in real life end with a stream of expressions like 'bye then', 'see you soon' and 'look after yourself', but in art we can either cut this down to a minimum or simply cut it out altogether, leaving the scene before the characters leave each other. (There are exceptions to every rule, however. The remarkable television series *The Royle Family* – writers, Caroline Aherne, Craig Cash and Henry Normal – seems to include every last banality of entrance and exit, not to mention long periods of gawping at television, interrupted only by cups of tea and visits to the toilet. But it should be noted, firstly, that this apparently extreme naturalism conceals art – particularly the art of some wonderful one-liners which *appear* totally unforced – and, secondly, that this series is to a large extent *about* the humour-through-banality of these characters.)

It is not only beginnings and endings, though, which can be uninteresting from a dramatic point of view. In real conversation there may well be all sorts of other everyday material which adds nothing and merely slows down what in dramatic terms we would call the action. Of course, if some of the trivia – 'Would you like a cup of tea?' – can be turned to advantage, all very well. In *A Few*

Kind Words, a Derbyshire ex-miner is visiting his daughter and son-in-law; the old man is asked how many sugars he would like in his tea and replies, 'Four please. Allus had a sweet tooth. Oh, not in them little cups, one in that.' Here the trivia has been used to make a point about their differing lifestyles: he initially assumes that he is being offered tea in a mug, as he would drink it at home. Very often, though, it is wiser simply to cut all such material.

To return to the dull piece of dialogue above, then: it should probably have begun a few lines before the introduction of the topic of the wedding, assuming that this topic was going to develop into something of interest. That would at least have spared us the wait while Jane visits the toilet. (Toilet scenes seem to be quite in vogue at present, but this one – or, rather, the lack of it, as we do not go there with her and nothing happens in her absence – is pointless.) Certainly, in 'real life' Pauline might well sit doing nothing for a couple of minutes awaiting the return of her friend, but that is a *very* long time for an audience to be doing the same! For our purposes this verisimilitude is not enough.

So scripted dialogue should be concise, relative to dialogue in 'real life'. This applies to all the script media, but particularly to film (even more than television), where we expect the visuals to do a great deal more of the work. *Often in film, the scenes are also often extremely short – there may be only one or two speeches to a scene (and some scenes, of course, have no speeches at all), so being concise is absolutely vital*. But even in radio scripts, dominated by dialogue though they are, dialogue must never be woolly or long-winded.

This leads us to the concept of *selective naturalism*. Selective naturalism is the style of writing which attempts to faithfully imitate dialogue as we normally speak it, but, unnoticed, manages to omit all those passages – not only beginnings and endings but also all sorts of other uninteresting sections – which would add nothing to the production. For it is not enough merely to imitate life: scripts are not straight, one-for-one imitations of slabs of life. In selective naturalism they are crafted, moulded to *appear* as if they were. Even in soap operas, crammed as they are with tea-pourings and the like, there has been sufficient editing of naturalism for the story to keep its onward movement.

The appearance of naturalism

Let us look at a fine piece of writing in the style of selective naturalism, the opening of Arnold Wesker's stage play *I'm Talking About Jerusalem*:

> *September 1946.*
> *Norfolk. A house in the middle of the fields. We see the large kitchen of the house, the garden, and the end of an old barn. (DAVE and ADA SIMMONDS are just moving in. Boxes and cases are strewn around. DAVE and two REMOVAL MEN are manoeuvring a large wardrobe, 1930 type, from a lorry offstage. ADA is unpacking one of the cases. SARAH KAHN, her mother, is buttering her bread on a table, and from a portable radio comes a stirring part of Beethoven's Ninth Symphony. RONNIE KAHN, Ada's brother, is standing on a box conducting both the music and the movement of people back and forth. DAVE – unlike ADA and RONNIE – speaks with a slight cockney accent.)*

RONNIE: Gently now. Don't rush it. You're winning.

DAVE: Instead of standing there and giving orders why don't you give a bloody hand?

RONNIE: You don't need any more hands. I'm organising you, I'm inspiring you.

DAVE: Jesus Christ it's heavy, it's heavy. Drop it a minute.

RONNIE: Lower it gently – mind the edges, it's a work of art.

DAVE: I'll work of art you. And turn that radio off – I can cope with Beethoven but not both of you.

RONNIE: (*turns off radio*) What are you grumbling for? I've been shlapping things to and fro up till now, haven't I? Only as it's the last piece I thought I'd exercise my talents as a foreman. Don't I make a good foreman? (*calling*) Hey, Mother, don't I make a good foreman?

SARAH: (*coming from kitchen*) What've you lost?

RONNIE: Listen to her! What've you lost! She's just like her daughter, she can't hear a thing straight. Watch this. Hey, Ada! The sea's not far away you know.

ADA: You can't have any because I haven't put the kettle on yet.

RONNIE: Lunatic family.

DAVE: Come on. We'll never get done. Ready?
> (*They bend to lift the wardrobe. SARAH returns to kitchen.*)
RONNIE: Heave – slowly – don't strain – heave.
1st R.M.: Where's it going?
DAVE: Through the kitchen and upstairs.

The first thing that hits us about this is that the dialogue is full of so much life. We are dropped straight into the middle of the scene, a busy scene – into the middle of dialogue, the middle of the action. The dialogue feels generally unforced and pleasingly messy, capturing domesticity without being in the least bit dull. Even in these few lines we begin to see the differences in character between Ronnie and Dave but, importantly, it is the actions – their contributions to the moving of the furniture and their responses to it – that give us this opportunity. The dialogue is about *doing* – there is a genuine need for it; it is not people sitting around talking for the sake of it. Only the joke about Ada's poor hearing feels a little forced – it works too well, and perhaps we sense the author's hand. We will return to this extract in Chapter 4, but for now we should note it as an example of a certain approach to naturalism, very much of a piece with that of Osborne's *Look Back in Anger* and other scripts of that period.

Now let us look at another script which might also be considered to be written in the style of selective naturalism, Mike Leigh's film *Secrets and Lies*:

> *A little later. CYNTHIA, HORTENSE, ROXANNE, PAUL and JANE are sitting round the table. MAURICE is busy at the barbecue, whilst MONICA bustles about, serving everybody.*

ROXANNE: So you work with my Mum, yeah?
HORTENSE: Yeah.
ROXANNE: Not on the machines?
HORTENSE: (*laughing slightly*) No.
CYNTHIA: You comin' round tomorrow night, Paul?
ROXANNE: Mum!
PAUL: Well it's –
CYNTHIA: Eh?
ROXANNE: We're goin' out!
> (MONICA *starts collecting everyone's finished corn-cobs.*)

MONICA: (*To* HORTENSE) Just take this.

CYNTHIA: Well, you'll come round before'and, won't you, 'ave a drink? It's 'er twenty-first.

ROXANNE: It's no big deal!

CYNTHIA: Well, I ain't given you your present yet!

MONICA: Thank you, Jane.

> (MAURICE *puts down a dish on the table.*)

MAURICE: Chicken drumsticks...

CYNTHIA: D'you want some salad, sweet'eart?

HORTENSE: Yes, please.

CYNTHIA: I'll get you some. (*She goes over to a separate serving table.*)

MONICA: Are you doing something special tomorrow night, you two?

ROXANNE: No, down the pub as usual.

MONICA: Oh?

JANE: (*To* MAURICE) Do you use fingers?

MAURICE: Use what you like! Use your feet if you want!

> (JANE *giggles.*)

MONICA: You've a knife and fork there, Jane.

JANE: 'T's a bit late, now.

Here, too, we have a scene full of life, and we have been dropped into the middle of it. (The opening stage direction, 'A little later', of course, is aimed at the director, actors and crew – we must be able to see that the meal has progressed since the previous scene.) By comparison, even the extract from *I'm Talking About Jerusalem* – excellent though it is – seems a little stilted. Leigh works through improvisation, only producing a script after many weeks of working with his actors, and developing particularly both characterisation and relationships. This complexity and apparent spontaneity shows through: each line arises naturally from the relationships and dynamics of the particular situation, yet there is an effortlessness about it – none of the lines seems forced. Each individual has their own agenda, while every line reminds us of a character trait (even the ambiguity of Monica's 'Oh?', with its shaded disapproval, or Paul's 'Well, it's – ', Paul being one of the least verbally communicative characters in film literature). Here is no trace of the authorial hand. The effect of the dialogue in this film is cumulative; points are not rammed home to us but rather our understanding of characters is allowed to grow as the film progresses. A line such as Monica's 'You've a knife and fork there, Jane' is restrained, yet in context contributes to our understanding of Monica's obsession with correctness and appearances.

Mike Leigh is not alone in using elements of improvisation in his scripts. For the film *Gosford Park* the director Robert Altman did not start from improvisation, but – with the full approval of the writer, Julian Fellowes – encouraged his cast to improvise around the already brilliant script. The result is stunning.

Now let us look at an extract from the television series *The Bill*. We join the episode at the end of a chase after a young woman. P.C. Barry Stringer has been doing all the hard work, running after her while the other officers are in cars:

13. EXT. STATION FORECOURT. DAY. 9.08AM

FROM OPPOSITE DIRECTIONS THE PANDA CAR AND AREA CAR ARRIVE. THEY BOTH STOP, THOUGH THE AREA CAR SWERVES TO BLOCK THE ALLEY EXIT. ALL FOUR OFFICERS GET OUT (STAMP AND DATTA FROM THE AREA CAR, QUINNAN AND FORD FROM THE PANDA CAR). AS THEY DO SO THE WOMAN COMES RUNNING FROM THE WASTEGROUND. SHE VIRTUALLY RUNS STRAIGHT INTO STAMP'S ARMS.

STAMP: (TO FORD AND QUINNAN, WHILE HOLDING ONTO THE WOMAN) What kept you? (TO WOMAN) You're nicked. What's your name?

NOW ALL AT THE SAME TIME FORD IS TALKING TO QUINNAN, STAMP IS CAUTIONING THE WOMAN AND DATTA IS SPEAKING INTO HER RADIO. WE FIND OURSELVES CLOSEST TO FORD AND QUINNAN. BEHIND ALL THIS WE SEE STRINGER ARRIVE, BREATHLESS.

FORD: What goes in must come out, eh?
QUINNAN: Yeah, well I didn't say where, did I?
DATTA: (SIMULTANEOUS WITH THE ABOVE) (INTO RADIO) Sierra Oscar from 181, receiving?

PETERS: (THROUGH RADIO) Go ahead, Norika.

STAMP: (SIMULTANEOUS WITH THE ABOVE) I am arresting you on suspicion of theft. You don't have to say anything but anything you do say may be given in evidence –

STRINGER: Hold on! She's my body!

STAMP: Too late me old son.

QUINNAN: You been out jogging Barry?

STRINGER: She's <u>my body!</u>

THE WOMAN, WILLIAMS, LOOKING FRIGHTENED, TURNS TO STAMP.

WILLIAMS: What's he mean?

SINCE STRINGER'S INTERVENTION, DATTA HAS BEEN SPEAKING TO PETERS.

DATTA: (INTO RADIO, SIMULTANEOUS WITH THE ABOVE) We've caught her, Sarge, outside Dorney Road Station.

PETERS: (THROUGH RADIO) Great stuff! And the goods?

NOW, AFTER WILLIAMS' 'EH?' AND BEFORE STAMP CAN ANSWER, DATTA CALLS OVER –

DATTA: Where's her bag?

EVERYONE STOPS

STAMP: Where's your bag, love?

WILLIAMS: What bag?

STRINGER: She chucked it out behind some bushes.

DATTA: (SMILING MISCHIEVOUSLY, INTO RADIO) Stringer's just going to recover the stolen goods, Sarge.

STRINGER IS FURIOUS.

Superficially, this has some resemblances to the extract from *Secrets and Lies*. Here again we have a carefully orchestrated piece of dialogue, a number of conversations taking place together, synchronised with action. As in the preceding extract, not only the director but also the writer has to be aware of what we – the audience – will and will not be able to hear. (Leigh, the writer/director, gives no stage direction to indicate which characters are nearest to the audience, but in filming simply has the camera positioned at one end of the patio and leaves it there, giving a rare effect of all the conversations having equal prominence.) However, whereas meaning is always transparent – at least superficially – in Mike Leigh, in *The Bill* there is frequent use of police jargon (for example, 'My body...', 'Sierra Oscar from 181...'). This is there partly because it is, on occasions, what the police would say; but it is also there to add a certain flavour. Very often it is not particularly important whether the audience actually understands the jargon: its purpose is to *be* jargon, to impress upon the audience that they are being given a glimpse of a separate, enclosed world with its own language. Often in this sort of series there will also be an element of 'clever-cleverness' in the dialogue, again not because this is how police officers necessarily talk to each other, but because this is how we enjoy *thinking* that they talk to each other. The dialogue is written to live up to our expectations. Just as the normal day-to-day activities of police officers (all those forms to fill in...) are much less exciting than any single episode of *The Bill*, so in real life their dialogue is often very dull; in the television series it invariably has a little added spice. In *Secrets and Lies* the dialogue really does reflect much of ordinary conversation – we are given the opportunity to focus on the verbal limitations of a number of the characters – while in *The Bill* nothing is allowed to stay ordinary for very long. This is a police series which prides itself upon being true to life (and in many respects, such as the accuracy of police procedures, it is indeed impressively accurate); yet certainly, in its dialogue, it presents what is in fact an illusion of gritty naturalism.

In each of the examples above there are lines which appear not to contribute very much at all – the trivia of our verbal interaction – yet none of the scenes comes to a halt under the weight of normality. This is partly because each of these scenes relies heavily upon action. Things happen. While of course there is a place in drama for speech set outside a context of action, it is sometimes hard to keep a momentum in dialogue which is only about itself, which is only about the subject of the conversation. But in each of these scenes there is a strong element of *business* – the physical moving of furniture into the house, the cooking, serving, eating and clearing away of the barbecue, the arrival one after the other of a host of police officers and a suspect.

Humour and the ordinary

In each of the given extracts, humour is used to lighten the proceedings. Datta mischievously adds insult to injury by sending the already exhausted Stringer – who has just lost his 'body' – to retrieve the stolen goods; Dave is forced to respond to Ronnie's conducting of both the Beethoven and the moving of the furniture; we are gently amused by the bluntness of Cynthia and Roxanne, the stifling correctness of Monica and the pleasantries of Maurice. Some of this humour is direct, some subtle; all of it adds to our enjoyment of the scenes, and humour is particularly useful in adding flavour to everyday exchanges which might otherwise be somewhat bland.

Here, then, we have three examples of selective naturalism – three out of thousands of possible examples of what might be called 'filleted reality'. Not only are we not given the whole scene – beginnings and endings, or both, have been cut off – but the dialogue itself has been distilled while giving the impression of being precisely the opposite. The phrases and actions of normality are all there, but never in the quantity, at the length or with the sheer tedium of much of real life. Everything, in fact, serves a purpose. It is when that purpose becomes too apparent that danger arises, as we shall see in the following chapter.

4. Don't Make it Work Too Hard!

The story without a narrator

Most of the words of a script consist of dialogue, and usually there is no narrator. How, then, is information imparted? In a novel or a short story the narrator will often fill in the background, perhaps telling us about the past life of characters, describing physical appearances or presenting the setting of the story – the town, the institution, the workplace or wherever. All this information, of course, helps us to visualise and understand the characters, their speeches and their actions. The narrator will sometimes be a character, but more often will be an impersonal, third-person, omniscient being, able to tell us people's most private secret thoughts – perhaps even their unconscious motivations. This narrator can tell us everything we could possibly need to know – and in fact may even tell us some things we would rather not know. The narrator is our guide, the mediator between the fictional world of the characters and our own world.

So how on earth can story-telling – and drama is a form of story-telling – survive without such a tremendously useful entity as a narrator? For in most drama there is no such guide, no such mediator: there is no teller of the story. One answer to the problem is, simply, to use a narrator after all – this use in drama is the subject of Chapter 9 – but without one, how are its functions fulfilled? With only dialogue, action and visuals (and in radio drama not even that), how is the story told?

The worst solution

The worst solution to this problem is one adopted by many inexperienced scriptwriters: to cram the dialogue full of all sorts of information. The writer – who has perhaps been used to having recourse to a narrator when writing short stories or novels – is close to panic in the absence of this prop; he or she assumes that drama should aspire to the condition of narrative (by which is meant here the short story or novel). This is the basic mistake: in fact, no compensation for the absence of a narrator is necessary, since narrative and drama are two distinct forms with their own strengths – neither need imitate the other. But our writer does not realise this, and instead uses dialogue to have characters telling each other all sorts of things which might sit quite comfortably with a narrator; stuffed into speech they produce only artificiality.

There is no narrator in life

The novel has changed a great deal over the last hundred years or so. Now there are novels with one, two, three or more narrators, with hardly a narrator at all or with narrators who cannot be trusted. Nevertheless, much of our reading is from an earlier time, when many narrators were omniscient, leading you carefully through the jungle of events within the covers. A narrator in, say, a Jane Austen novel might not tell us everything – she does give us the opportunity to work some things out for ourselves – and might load many of her comments with irony, but much of the pleasure of reading such a narrative comes from the quality of her (the narrator's) interpretation of speeches, feelings and actions of the characters. Despite the profound effects of modernism and post-modernism in our own times, there is still much literature written in this tradition. This is fine, but as scriptwriters we should recognise that our business really is quite different (this also explains the rarity of the totally satisfying stage or screen adaptation of a novel). We present a world without a mediator, a world in which the audience has to make what sense it can of all that is said or done, much as people do outside the theatre. There is, after all, no narrator in life. And this approach brings with it many advantages. The audience has to work harder, and that in itself produces a certain involvement: they want to know the answers to a mass of questions and so they have to pay attention to get those answers. No-one is simply going to give them to them. Of course, this can be taken too far: the script might provide so little information as to make it impossible for the audience to come to any conclusions at all; this can become merely annoying – the audience may begin to feel too much the play-thing of the author. The basic point remains, however: drama handles life in a different way from narrative, and the dialogue within drama should not try to compensate for the lack of a narrator.

In the film *French Kiss* (writer, Adam Brooks) the change in attitude of Kate (Meg Ryan) towards France is central to the meaning of the script. She starts by hating it and ends by adoring it, and this is an indicator of her love not only for her new French partner but also for what he represents – family, the land, a settled future. Yet this information – her change in attitude – is never *directly* expressed in dialogue. That is not to say that the change is handled with great subtlety: she begins by singing 'I hate Paris in the Springtime' and ends by having 'I love Paris' emblazoned on her t-shirt: the contrast is hardly made difficult to spot! But this change is never commented upon in generalised terms either by herself or by other characters: it is always presented in specifics. Her loathing for French cheese changes to attempts at enjoyment; she starts to appreciate the beauty of the French countryside; and – perhaps most important of all in symbolic terms – she takes in the Eiffel Tower, which initially is continually hidden from her. Had this been a novel, the narrator might have stated the fact that her attitude to France had altered (though a subtle narrator actually might not); in the film the audience is left to deduce it; it is not 'dumped' into the dialogue.

'Is that your green-eyed blonde younger sister crossing the busy dual carriageway over there?'

A poor scriptwriter, however, does not appreciate any of this. Nor does he or she realise that much of the information being forced into the dialogue is in fact utterly unnecessary. In a radio play, for example, we do not need one character to describe to another the physical appearance of a third character (or – worse – of each other!); such observations might be appropriate for a narrator in a story, but in a drama it is almost certainly dead weight, only holding up the action. At its worst this type of dialogue can lead to characters telling each other what they already know, just for the benefit of the audience. The subtitle above – 'Is that your green-eyed blonde sister crossing the busy dual carriageway over there?' – would of course be ridiculous as a piece of dialogue, but it is not actually much more extreme than many such nuggets embedded in scripts received by theatres and broadcasting companies every day (though it has to be said that radio tends to invite more of this type of error than do the other media, as many writers – wrongly – assume that in radio not only must we compensate for the lack of narrator, but also for the lack of visuals).

Characters must only tell each other what they feel that they need to tell each other; they must never tell each other what the *writer* feels that he or she needs to tell the audience. Any information to be imparted must be presented in such a way as to meet this first criterion. Failure in this respect means that a confusion has arisen between the agendas of the characters and the agenda of the author.

However, I should add just one rider to this in the case of radio. On stage, or on either the small or the big screen, a character does not cease to be there if he or she is not speaking. On radio, however, that is virtually what happens. Radio creates a picture in our heads, and that picture changes as the scene moves along. So, near the start of each new scene, each character should speak, so that we can include them in the mental picture (or, if they do not speak, their presence must be referred to, though this is not as powerful a signal as speech). Furthermore, each character should then say a line or two at *fairly regular intervals* – about once per page – or else they will drop out of the mental picture, and then, if they do speak – after, say, three pages of being silent – the effect is surreal, as though the character has suddenly shoved his or her head through the wall to say something. To this extent, then, the writer does have an agenda which has to be inflicted on the characters somewhat artificially, and carrying this off by always giving the impression that each character *needs* to each speak each line is a particular skill of the radio scriptwriter.

Some terrible dialogue

However, our poor scriptwriter does not appreciate any of this, about confusion of agendas of the characters and of the writer. Not only does this writer inject all sorts of inappropriate information into the dialogue, but he or she also hankers after another function of the traditional narrator. In a novel or short story the narrator will not only set the scene but will also interpret events at the moment of their happening, inviting us to come to particular conclusions about whatever is said or done. The inexperienced writer will try to force dialogue into performing a comparable role. Something like the following might result:

ALICE and CATH are both seated in ALICE's living room.

ALICE: So your boss is completely obsessed with punctuality.
CATH: Completely.
ALICE: And he tells you off when you're even a minute late.
CATH: Even a second.
ALICE: He hasn't been in the job long, has he.
CATH: No.
ALICE: About three months.
CATH: That's right.
ALICE: So did you prefer your old boss?
CATH: Loads. He was always so kind.
ALICE: Oh I remember. He sent you those flowers when you were in hospital, didn't he.
CATH: Yes. And I was only there two days.
ALICE: Oh and he was always good about your time off in lieu, wasn't he.
CATH: Which Mr Hambley never is. He always puts pressure on me – makes me feel as if I'm not really entitled to it.
ALICE: But you are.
CATH: Of course I am.
       slight pause
CATH: Your boss is okay though, isn't she.
ALICE: Barbara? Yeah, she's great.
CATH: She really takes on board what you've got to say, doesn't she.
ALICE: Exactly.
       slight pause
CATH: You know, it's so long since we've talked together... I really like it. We've really got a close relationship. It's almost as if I could read your thoughts sometimes.
ALICE: Me too.

This is pretty terrible stuff. The two characters are each telling each other information which the other already knows, with the thinnest of pretexts, merely to inform the audience; and then Cath invites the audience to come to a conclusion about their relationship. Of course, in a more subtle script, Cath's final speech could be viewed differently – we might see that they do not in fact have a close relationship, although Cath believes that they do. Alternatively, perhaps Cath could be trying to give an impression of closeness to Alice while not believing it herself, and Alice might or might not be taken in by this. In the context of this awful dialogue, however, we are tempted to take everything at face value, as there are no other signs of subtlety.

No spoon-feeding

So, how might such a piece of dialogue have been better scripted? There are of course a multitude of ways in which it could be rewritten, depending upon what the writer wanted to achieve. Some of the information could be omitted altogether, while other pieces might remain but only because the characters are given credible motivation for mentioning them. Here is one alternative version:

> *CATH and ALICE are both seated in ALICE's living room.*

CATH: I'm just going to have to leave. Find another job.
ALICE: What?
CATH: Well he's mad. He's completely obsessed with punctuality. It's driving me round the bend.
ALICE: Have you told him?
CATH: I mean, if I'm just a minute late –
ALICE: (*overlapping*) But have you told him, that he's being –
CATH: (*overlapping*) I think he's trying to establish his authority or something. No of course I haven't told him – he's my boss.
ALICE: I'd tell Barbara.
CATH: But he's not Barbara. I mean Brian was always so kind – flowers and whatever –
ALICE: Maybe he'll calm down.
CATH: Or maybe he won't. Even time off in lieu – he makes me feel as if I'm not really entitled to it.
ALICE: Well you do...
> *A look from CATH, but ALICE carries on.*
ALICE: You did use to take quite a lot of time –

CATH: No more than I was entitled to! You're meant to be able to take time off – it's in lieu – you know?
ALICE: Yeah, yeah.
　　slight pause
CATH: Anyway, I'd better be off.
　　A nod from ALICE.

This is a considerable improvement. Alice is no longer feeding Cath with all sorts of information which Cath already knows. Instead, Cath has been provided with a motivation for telling us about the situation – it is so bad that she is thinking of leaving her job. In addition, the conversation no longer resembles ping-pong: Alice's early interjections are all but ignored by Cath, who only replies when she has got her initial anger and frustration off her chest. In the first version everything was explained – the flowers were sent to the hospital although she was only there for three days, and Barbara is a good boss because she listens to everything her juniors tell her. In this version, though, there is some shorthand – the flowers are mentioned with the assumption that Alice will remember the details, and *no further details are provided for the audience*. (There may or may not be another reference elsewhere in the script which, together with this, might make things clearer.) This rids the exchange of artificiality, and, besides, the audience does not in fact *need* to know all these details. Similarly the mention of Alice's boss, Barbara, now relies on them both knowing her qualities – the audience is not spoon-fed.

In the first version, the two of them agreed about everything; now there is a little needle between them, culminating in Alice's hesitant, 'Well you do... You did use to take quite a lot of time – ' and Cath's annoyed response. This shade of conflict adds interest in itself, but it also lends a whole new ambiguity to the scene. No longer can we assume the correctness of Cath's version of events: perhaps she does take time off without justification, so perhaps too she is continually late, and her boss's reprimands are justified. This ambiguity – our *not knowing* one way or the other – keeps us pulled into the action: we want to find out the truth. It also makes the relationship between the two characters more involving. Continual agreement (like continual disagreement) can be tiresome; most relationships involve subtle shades of agreement and conflict, so this piece of dialogue both reflects reality more accurately and is more likely to hold our attention as a piece of drama. Again, we want to find out the truth, in this case the truth of the precise nature of their relationship – so we want to see more of it, to see how it develops. Similarly, in this second version we are fortunately spared Cath's summing up of their relationship – we are left to come to some provisional conclusions ourselves, which is much more interesting than being told. Of course, there is no reason why a character (with credible motivation) should not sum up the nature of a relationship or of a conversation, but, as noted above, it should not be presented in such a way as merely to invite straightforward acceptance by the audience.

Now let us have one more stab at this scene. We have already made the dialogue more messy, we have added shades of conflict and ambiguity, we have avoided feeding the audience with information and we have not told the audience what to think. Now let us add a little business. Of course, we could move the scene from the domestic setting altogether, but even without doing this we can certainly add further interest, perhaps by moving it from living room to kitchen, where there is rather more to do.

> CATH and ALICE in ALICE's kitchen. Alice is making bread, kneading the dough.

CATH: I'm just going to have to leave. Find another job.
ALICE: What?
CATH: Well he's mad –
ALICE: Pass us the flour, could you.
CATH: – completely obsessed with punctuality. It's driving me round the bend.
ALICE: Have you told him?
CATH: I mean, if I'm just a minute late –
ALICE: (*overlapping*) But have you told him, that he's being –
CATH: (*overlapping*) I think he's trying to establish his authority or something. No of course I haven't told him – he's my boss.
ALICE: I'd tell Barbara.
CATH: Yeah well he's not Barbara, is he. Why do you bother to make bread, Alice? It's just as good from the supermarket.
ALICE: Thanks very much.
CATH: And it's probably cheaper. It's certainly less messy.
no reply

CATH: I mean Brian was always so kind – flowers and whatever –
ALICE: Maybe this new fella'll calm down.
CATH: Or maybe he won't. Even time off in lieu – he makes me
   , feel as if I'm not really entitled to it.
   ALICE stops kneading for a moment.
ALICE: Well you do...
   *A look from CATH, but ALICE carries on speaking and
   resumes kneading.*
ALICE: You did use to take quite a lot of time –
CATH: No more than I was entitled to! You're meant to be able to
   take time off – it's <u>in lieu</u> – you know?
ALICE: Yeah, yeah.
   lengthy pause
CATH: So... will that really rise?
ALICE: Should do, yeah.
   slight pause
CATH: Anyway, I'd better be off.
   A nod from ALICE.

Displacing our emotions

In the above, the action of making bread is not merely a bit of business to add some interest to the scene: rather, the business feeds back into the meaning of the scene itself. Cath is annoyed with Alice, initially for her comment 'I'd tell Barbara', which seems to fail to acknowledge that Barbara is a much easier boss to talk to than her own new boss; but rather than expressing this directly to Alice she does so indirectly, instead criticising her bread-making. This is very common: we often displace our emotions; if we cannot cope with dealing with them head-on (perhaps because it would create too destructive a confrontation) we transfer them to someone or something else. In this case, Cath's comments about Alice's bread-making are substituting for any comments Cath might otherwise have made about Alice's attitude to her (Cath's) problem. Of course, the scriptwriter does not have to enter into a psychological analysis of precisely what is going on on all such occasions; rather, he or she must develop a *feel* for this sort of behaviour and incorporate it into dialogue as a matter of course. There are dangers, though. If handled too heavily – if in this case the bread were called upon to act clearly as a symbol – it can appear laboured and artificial. A light touch is generally preferable.

Towards the end of this version, after the lengthy pause to allow herself to become more calm, Cath returns to the subject of the bread – 'So... will that really rise?' Perhaps she feels here that her previous anger has been disproportionate. She uses the bread now as a means of being conciliatory. The tone is ambiguous, though – the question 'So... will that really rise?' might be mildly admiring of Alice's skill (it is an acknowledgement that Alice knows how to make bread, and Cath doesn't), but at the same time retains a slight edge of doubt, of not trusting her judgement. These are the subtleties – never to be analysed by the audience, only to be felt – which the scriptwriter must aim for.

As the title of this chapter suggests, good dialogue – though it does of course accomplish a great deal – should not be made to *work too hard* (as in the first version of the Alice and Cath scene above). In particular, it should not be made to work hard in ways for which it is inappropriate. The audience, on the other hand, *should* be made to work, and sometimes quite hard. Frequently, one can simply transfer the burden of work from the dialogue to the audience. Such a transference is almost always beneficial.

Two small examples from the work of Arthur Miller come to mind. At the start of the second act of *Death of A Salesman*, Willy Loman is having his coffee cup refilled by Linda, his wife. We have already witnessed profound problems within the family, as well as Willy's overpowering consciousness of failure. The first spoken line of the Act is Willy's: 'Wonderful coffee. Meal in itself.' This modest little line sums up Willy's change of attitude at that moment. Once more he is positive, optimistic (although he does not say that *he* is feeling wonderful – rather, that the coffee is wonderful). Yet even in this unassuming line there is a certain overstatement – can a coffee really be a meal in itself? – which reminds us not to trust his feelings entirely; he believes what he wants to believe. Clearly, the audience is not intended to analyse this innocuous line, this response to a bit of domestic business, yet the effect is there nevertheless, and expressed through this substitution more eloquently than any direct statement.

At the start of the second act of Miller's *The Crucible*, John Proctor is alone. We already know that he has been unfaithful to his wife, and that he regrets it. The Act begins with him taking a sample of the rabbit stew his wife has made; he is not entirely satisfied. He adds some salt. At this point there are no lines of dialogue referring to this at all, but a piece of domestic business has taken on a quality of symbolism, and in a quiet, understated way. It is his wife whom he finds lacking in flavour, and although he does regret his infidelity he still wishes she had, as it were, more salt. Once again, stated in this way this may sound absurd, but the symbolism does have its effect, whether at a conscious or unconscious level. Of course, it is not the function of this book to attempt a detailed analysis of how symbolism works; it is its relationship with dialogue that is important. So the point for us is that this is not put into words. At no point does Proctor state, 'I wish you were more exciting!' Rather, when he starts to eat, he comments to Linda that the dish is well seasoned; she is pleased, telling him that she has taken great care with the meal. The dialogue here is used to develop the symbolism, but not to express the meaning directly; his dissatisfaction, his attempt to compensate for it and disguise it, her wish to please him and her incapacity to do so are all expressed through the rabbit stew. Direct statement injected into the dialogue would have been much less effective.

In Athol Fugard's moving play '*Master Harold*'... *and the boys*, set in the South Africa of 1950, split down the middle by apartheid, much of the dialogue focuses on very visible business: dancing. The three characters, Sam, Willie and the young white man, Hally, all dance, and it is this *activity* which allows the scriptwriter to let his characters express all that they want to about how their world functions. Towards the end of the play Sam makes a passionate but simple speech about dancing. He tells the others that they are all bumping into each other, that we all bump into each other, that nations keep bumping into each other, and despite all the pain inflicted we don't seem to be able to stop doing it – but it's got to stop. We have to stop always dancing like beginners. A piece of dialogue which might easily have seemed preachy or artificial is given both plausibility and resonance by being so firmly attached to business – in this case his attempts at teaching the others to dance. The meanings in the dialogue are not transferred to dance, but neither are they merely demonstrated by the dance: instead, they actually *are* the dance.

Dialogue and events

When dialogue is made to work too hard, sometimes it is because it is being asked to take the place of a narrator. However, it can also happen for other reasons. The scriptwriter must never forget that, however important the dialogue, things must also actually happen. *Dialogue must not be made to substitute for events.* The mistake can be made in one of two ways: events are either omitted altogether, or they consistently take place offstage and have to be reported onstage.

There is always an offstage (or 'out of vision') world. Whatever a script presents, there are always events which are referred to – or which the audience simply assumes to have happened – but which are not actually shown. (In fact, a number of playwrights have toyed with this, notably – though in very different ways – Michael Frayn in *Noises Off*, in which the backstage of a theatre performance becomes the onstage; and Tom Stoppard in *Rosencrantz and Guildenstern Are Dead*, in which the central characters are two minor characters from *Hamlet*, so that all the major events of that play happen offstage.) Whatever is not shown must be told; there is always a choice between telling and showing (or omitting altogether); a balance has to be struck, and one of the consequences of failing to strike that balance correctly is to overload the dialogue.

Telling and showing

Showing is almost always more vivid, more memorable than telling. By 'showing' I do not mean, of course, that no dialogue is used, but rather that we witness an event itself – including the dialogue – rather than being told about it *through* the dialogue. At the start of *The Tempest*, for example, we are shown the storm at sea – dialogue and action. The sailors are already yelling above the noise of the storm; asked where the Master is, the Boatswain yells 'Do you not hear him?', meaning that they are being mastered by the wind. We are thrown immediately into action, and into dialogue in the context of action. The sailors are trying to keep the ship afloat while at the same time having to deal with those Lords aboard who are getting in their way:

On a ship at sea. A tempestuous noise of thunder and lightning heard.
Enter a SHIP-MASTER and a BOATSWAIN, severally.

MASTER: Boatswain!

BOATSWAIN: Here, master: what cheer?

MASTER: Good, speak to the mariners: fall to't, yarely, or we run ourselves aground: bestir, bestir.
    [*Exit*]
    Enter MARINERS.

BOATSWAIN: Heigh, my hearts! cheerly, cheerly, my hearts! yare, yare! Take in the topsail; tend to the master's whistle. – Blow, till thou burst thy wind, if room enough!
    Enter ALONSO, SEBASTIAN, ANTONIO, FERDINAND, GONZALO and others.

ALONSO: Good boatswain, have care. Where's the master? Play the men.

BOATSWAIN: I pray now, keep below.

ANTONIO: Where is the master, boson?

BOATSWAIN: Do you not hear him? You mar our labour. Keep your cabins: you do assist the storm.

GONZALO: Nay, good, be patient.

BOATSWAIN: When the sea is Hence! What care these roarers for the name of king? To cabin: silence! trouble us not.

GONZALO: Good, yet remember whom thou hast aboard.

BOATSWAIN: None that I love more than myself. You are a counsellor; if you command these elements to silence, and work the peace of the present, we will not hand a rope more; use your authority; if you cannot, give thanks that you have lived so long, and make yourself ready in your cabin for the mischance of the hour, if it so hap. Cheerly, good hearts! Out of our way, I say.

And so the scene continues, culminating in the wrecking of the ship. This scene could, of course, have been told instead of being shown. After the event, one of the survivors could simply have related what had happened to someone else. However, this would have had none of the immediacy of actually being there, seeing and hearing the things as they take place. The second scene of *The Tempest*, though, is a complete contrast. It begins with a conversation of great length between Prospero and his daughter Miranda, in which Prospero tells her all the events of twelve years previously which led to their being on the ship which was wrecked. There are those who believe this scene is too static and ponderous, even tedious – that it is too much telling; what does seem certain is that Shakespeare only felt able to load this piece of dialogue with so massive a burden of telling because it followed a scene of such vivid showing.

To take one more example from Shakespeare, in *The Winter's Tale* a section which might have been expected to be one of the high points of the play – the Fifth Act reconciliation of Leontes and Camillo – is told rather than shown. The rift between these two has been at the heart of the play, yet the reconciliation happens offstage; we hear about it through dialogue which is crammed full of the retailing of information – one Gentleman telling another what the two Kings said to each other on finally being reunited. This may well lead the audience to feel disappointed, or even deprived. Why did the writer cheat us of being shown this scene? He has asked dialogue to do too much of the work. So why, then, did Shakespeare do this? There appear to be two reasons. The first is that we already know the two Kings are to be reconciled and we know how this has come about, so to witness the reconciliation itself might only be an anti-climax anyway, adding little new. The second, stronger reason appears to be that had Shakespeare not conveyed the reunion through 'telling' in the dialogue, this might indeed have seemed the climax of the play, while in fact the playwright wants to reserve this for the following scene, a surprise – the return of Hermione seemingly from the dead in the final scene of the play. Using the dialogue in the previous scene, then, to tell about the reconciliation rather than showing it has the effect of downgrading its effect, leaving the way clear for the real climax.

As these examples show, there is certainly a place for using dialogue to tell rather than to show, but the positioning of such dialogue in the script as a whole needs to be considered. There are notable exceptions (such as the story-telling at the heart of Conor McPherson's *The Weir* – but then this is a play *about* the telling of stories), but in general too much telling and not enough showing can lead members of the audience to feel that they are too far from the action that really matters.

Telling, showing and form

The relationship between telling and showing – and thus what is demanded of the dialogue – can be affected by decisions about the overall form of the script. Through film, television and much of modern theatre we have become very used to moving with ease from one setting to another. Indeed, there will often be sequences with little or no dialogue using five, ten or even twenty settings. In Shakespeare's time, too, it was commonplace for a script to demand that we move from the palace straight to the wood, to a cottage and then perhaps to a ship or a fairies' grotto. Between Elizabethan times and the twentieth century, however, there grew up a strong tradition of stage plays using only one, two or three inflexible sets, culminating in the great plays of Chekhov and Ibsen. (These are very much closer to observing the Aristotelian unities of time, place and action.) The tradition has continued on into our time, co-existing with other, freer forms. In this type of theatre it is not so much that we, the audience, see action in one different place after another as the need arises, but rather that the action is manipulated to come to whatever fixed setting (and set) has been decided upon by the playwright. Typically in this sort of play, then, there is a living room or perhaps a bedsit (or, in earlier times, a drawing room or sitting room) through which a succession of characters pass; the action has to be carefully contrived so that most of the important events take place here. Inevitably, though, it proves impossible to make everything happen before our eyes when the playwright has chosen to use a form which imposes such limitations. This has an effect on the dialogue, as it means that, unavoidably, a higher proportion of the speeches are reporting events that have happened offstage rather than dealing with events as they happen: there will almost certainly be more telling and less showing.

In the hands of a less than highly skilful playwright, this may produce dialogue which is rather dull (though in other hands, recounting events – telling a story, in effect – can be very funny or arresting); it also can place stress upon motivation for the dialogue. After all, when something is happening at that moment it is simply happening, but recounting something that has already happened elsewhere demands a particular motivation – whoever is telling it needs to have a convincing reason to pass it on; it must not sound as if it is there primarily for the sake of the audience. Thus, there is a relationship between the form chosen and the demands put upon the dialogue: the freer the form, the easier it is to show rather than tell; and the easier it is to show, the less likely it is that the dialogue will be asked to work too hard.

The script in which nothing happens

The relationship between showing and telling only really applies, of course, when there are events to show or tell in the first place. It is remarkable, however, how many scripts are written – and received by production companies – in which virtually nothing seems to happen at all. The dialogue is not made to do some of the work: it is made to do almost *all* of the work. Yet in responding to characters in scripts just as in real life, we learn most about them through what they *do*. Words, as they say, are cheap. People may say all sorts of things, yet do things which in fact fly in the face of their own words. Of course, the words teach us something – perhaps that this person is weak, or a hypocrite – but ultimately only because of the way in which they form a contrast with the actions. Words alone are not enough.

Typically, the sort of script in which nothing happens begins with characters outlining a situation (probably one with which the writer is personally familiar). This may take up a scene or two, but then what is the writer to do? The answer, in this sort of script, is to widen the canvas. It is as though the writer were a painter, whose characters describe a particular scenario in some detail so that the audience can see it very clearly; but having finished that canvas, the scriptwriter is then at a loss – all he or she can do is reach for a bigger frame and have the characters describe that wider context too. And after that? Widen it yet again, or perhaps have the characters take a magnifying glass to the picture and tell us about the minutiae. The problem is that this writer is using the wrong metaphor, thinking of drama as a picture when it should be thought of as *moving pictures*. Things must happen. In fact, *every scene must move the action on*. To fail to observe this rule is to put intolerable strain upon the dialogue. If nothing happens, and all we are left with is the dialogue (and, of course, the visuals), then that dialogue has to be quite stunningly poetic, or fascinating, or hilarious. It must be quite exceptional.

67

There are, in fact, examples of precisely that. In Alan Bennett's *Talking Heads*, all we are given is the talking heads of the title, but the characterisation and story-telling are so brilliant that we need nothing more. In Dylan Thomas's *Under Milk Wood*, too, there is very little development – it is little more than a great big picture of a village – but *what* a picture! The fact is, though, that few of us have the abilities of an Alan Bennett or a Dylan Thomas, yet to write successful scripts in which almost nothing happens requires nothing less. Mere mortals are far safer with other approaches.

Presenting the evidence

There is one further point to be made about dialogue and the relationship between telling and showing. An audience is rather like a jury. It is presented with a great deal of evidence about a case and comes to conclusions based on that evidence. Of course, some pieces of evidence may be missing – adding mystery – and much of the evidence may be ambiguous, or even open to utterly contradictory interpretations; the audience-jury must make do with whatever is supplied. But, just as in court there are some sorts of evidence which are not admissible – hearsay, in particular – so in drama the audience will become frustrated if there is too much hearsay – too much telling – and ultimately will not trust this evidence. We need to be shown things, not merely to be told about them, if we are to believe them.

I will now give you an example from a play of my own. *Betrayers* deals with attitudes of British – or more specifically English – people towards foreigners, and how these attitudes are related to our treatment of asylum-seekers. Beatrice, a Latin American, is married to Mike, an Englishman. They seem to function well as a couple, but we come to realise that their relationship is based upon his patronising of her and her acceptance of being patronised. This all becomes clear when Beatrice's brother, Esteban, arrives. Esteban becomes furious at what his sister has come to accept as normal, turning on both of them:

ESTEBAN: But all it was, for you, was colonialisation.
    Colonialisation!
MIKE: Oh good God –
BEATRICE: You're not being –

ESTEBAN: That's all it was. That's all it is! The kind Englishman saves the poor defenceless girl form the 'third world' from ever having to go back to that... that squalor. That's how you see it isn't it? She becomes your little colony. And in return all that you ask is that she must be grateful forever. And you are aren't you Beatrice.

A little later he continues in similar vein:

ESTEBAN: You have rescued this... this 'exotic' woman. That's what you have done. And you display her at your dinner parties, and we are all meant to admire you for it, just like Beatrice does. For your generosity.

The problem with the first draft of this play was that we were almost entirely *told* about this patronising; we were *shown* only the tiniest glimpses of it. Almost all the evidence for its existence lay in these speeches of Esteban. Here was dialogue certainly being made to work too hard. The audience may well have become impatient: why should they believe all this when they were not shown it? They were only being given Esteban's dialogue *about* it – which is the courtroom equivalent of hearsay evidence.

Of course, there may be times when we will want dialogue to present hearsay precisely because it is unreliable. We want to use the second-hand nature of this type of speech to introduce an element of doubt. For example, we are not shown two characters kissing, but rather one character tells another that he saw it happen. Here the dialogue replaces the action for us, but we do not know whether or not to believe the speaker. This can be very effective. Indeed, we may have a number of different characters telling us conflicting versions of events – we are never shown the event itself – and we are left to try to sort out which, if any, is telling the truth. However, this use of dialogue to tell, in a situation where the truth of an event or interpretation is at issue, is quite distinct from the use of dialogue to tell something which we simply want the audience to accept as true: it is in this latter case that the dialogue is being made to work too hard.

5. Beyond the Literal

Taking things at face value

We have already touched upon a variety of ways in which speech, both in real life and in scripts, is very often not literal. We do not use speech simply to say what we mean. In this chapter we focus on the ways in which dialogue is often used either to obscure or to completely distort meanings.

In poor dialogue the audience is invited to take everything at face value. In the first version of the Cath and Alice conversation in the previous chapter, for example, what we hear is what we get. The statements are bald, with virtually no 'side' or 'sub-text'; both information and feelings are communicated without us at any point being invited to think that there might be subtle motivations, any unstated thoughts, any ambiguity of meaning. Yet in real life, how often do we express ourselves in this way? Not often.

Subtle ambiguities

Good dialogue thrives on subtle ambiguities. Ambiguities invite the audience in, to try to clarify what exactly is going on, what exactly is meant, what exactly is felt. At the start of Caryl Churchill's haunting play *Far Away*, for example, initially the dialogue seems very straightforward – certainly the language itself is uncomplicated – and the meanings clear: but they are not. The girl Joan is telling Harper, her aunt, that she saw some strange things the previous night. She had climbed out of her bedroom window and watched events from up a tree. But every time Harper gives a reasonable explanation of what Joan had seen, Joan first appears to accept it but then quietly reveals another piece of information which shows Harper's explanation so far to have been untrue. This happens a number of times, with Harper's final explanation being that what Joan had actually seen was a party:

HARPER: Just a little party.

JOAN: Yes, because there wasn't just that one person.

HARPER: No, there'd be a few of his friends.

JOAN: There was a lorry.

HARPER: Yes, I expect there was.

JOAN: When I put my ear against the side of the lorry I heard crying inside.

HARPER: How could you do that from up in the tree?

JOAN: I got down from the tree. I went to the lorry after I looked in the window of the shed.

HARPER: There might be things that are not your business when you're a visitor in someone else's house.

JOAN: Yes, I'd rather not have seen. I'm sorry.

HARPER: Nobody saw you?

JOAN: They were thinking about themselves.

HARPER: I think it's lucky nobody saw you.

JOAN: If it's a party, why was there so much blood?

HARPER: There isn't any blood.

JOAN: Yes.

HARPER: Where?

JOAN: On the ground.

HARPER: In the dark? How would you see that in the dark?

JOAN: I slipped in it.

> *She holds up her bare foot.*
> I mostly wiped it off.

HARPER: That's where the dog got run over this afternoon.

JOAN: Wouldn't it have dried up?

HARPER: Not if the ground was muddy.

JOAN: What sort of dog?

HARPER: A big dog, a big mongrel.

JOAN: That's awful, you must be very sad, had you had him long?

HARPER: No, he was young, he ran out, he was never very obedi-
ent, a lorry was backing up.

JOAN: What was his name?

HARPER: Flash.

JOAN: What colour was he?

HARPER: Black with a bit of white.

JOAN: Why were the children in the shed?

HARPER: What children?

JOAN: Don't you know what children?

HARPER: How could you see there were children?
JOAN: There was a light on. That's how I could see the blood
  inside the shed. I could see the faces and which ones had
  blood on.

The writer could simply have had Joan declare to Harper what she
had seen, in one unbroken account. This way, though, we learn
about the events almost as Joan sees them, little by little, trying to
piece together what they mean. More importantly, this way a
major ambiguity emerges in the character of Joan. Is she simply a
naïve little girl, telling what she has seen, one thing at a time, and
asking for explanations? Or does she really know – or at least
somehow intuitively sense – what has been going on, and in this
case is the form of her release of information in fact a way of entic-
ing Harper into committing herself to more and more lies? Does
Joan at some point believe that a dog was run over, or even that
there was a dog at all? Initially, as she asks about the animal, it
seems that she does believe the story, and even sympathises, but
then when she tells her aunt that she saw the children's faces with
blood on them it is clear that she knew all along that there was no
dog. Or is it clear? Perhaps, even as the lies accumulate, she has
still been trying as hard as she could to believe everything she has
been told. The ambiguity of meaning draws us in.

Now let us examine a very different example, from Anthony
Minghella's wonderful screenplay for the film *The English Patient*
(based on the novel by Michael Ondaatje). The scenes which we
will look at happen during a pre-war Christmas party in North
Africa: we have already seen Almásy picking at a piece of cake,
removing the marzipan icing; Katharine is married to Clifton (also
referred to as Geoffrey).

But before reading the scenes, perhaps it would be useful to think
of them simply in terms of action. In essence, the scenes' actions are:

(1) Katharine and Almásy make love in a storeroom in an ambas-
sadorial Palace, while the party continues;
(2) Katharine's husband Clifton, having heard that Katharine is not
feeling well, is looking for her. He comes across Almásy in a corridor;
(3) Clifton finds Katharine in a side room, alone, and expresses his
concern for her.

So, these are the actions in the scenes. How might we script them?
This is Minghella's realisation:

Int. Storeroom. Ambassador's residence. Day.

A small storeroom inside the Palace – brooms, mops, cleaning equipment. Outside, the party is visible as opaque shadows through the bevelled glass of the ornate window. The sound of carols sung by the enlisted men gives way to a version of 'Silent Night' on a solitary bagpipe. Inside, ALMÁSY and KATHARINE make love in the darkness. It's as if the world has stopped and there's only their passion, overwhelming reason and logic and rules.

Int. Corridors. Ambassador's residence. Day.
A corridor. ALMÁSY appears and almost immediately collides with the man dressed as Santa Claus.

> CLIFTON
Have you seen Katharine?

> ALMÁSY
> *(taken aback)*
What?

> CLIFTON
> *(pulling down his beard)*
It's Clifton under here.

> ALMÁSY
Oh no, I haven't, sorry.

Int. Side room in Ambassador's residence. Day.
Geoffrey continues scouring the warren of tiny rooms that run off the central courtyard. He finds KATHARINE sitting in one, smoking, surrounded by oppressive and elaborate tiling. CLIFTON wonders briefly how ALMÁSY had missed KATHARINE.

> CLIFTON
Darling, I just heard. You poor sausage. Are you all right?

KATHARINE

I'm fine. I'm just hot.

CLIFTON

Lady H said she thought you might be pregnant.

KATHARINE

I'm not pregnant. I'm just hot. Too hot. Aren't you?

CLIFTON

I'm sweltering, actually.
(taking off his hat and beard)
Come on, I'll take you home.

KATHARINE
(close to tears)
Can't we really go *home*? I can't breathe. Aren't you dying for green, anything green, or rain. It's Christmas and it's all – oh, I don't know – if you asked me I'd go home tomorrow. If you wanted.

CLIFTON

Darling, you know we can't go home, there might be a war.

KATHARINE
(poking at his costume)
Oh, Geoffrey, you do so love a disguise.

CLIFTON

I do so love you.
(he kisses her head)
What do you smell of?

KATHARINE:
(horrified)
What?

CLIFTON

Marzipan! I think you've got marzipan in your hair! No wonder you're homesick.

Here, the dialogue achieves much more than merely facilitating a straightforward understanding of events.

The extract begins with a scene using no dialogue at all. What we see and hear – given here in the stage directions – tells us all that we need to know. We do not need either Almásy or Katharine to comment on the circumstances in which they are making love, as we see that they are squashed into a storeroom; neither of them has to say that there is something squalid about this, but equally neither of them has to comment on their desperation to do this, or on their overwhelming passion. The stage directions tell us about this, as readers, but as viewers we can see it in their actions. Nor is any dialogue used to remind us of the dangers. We see the party 'as opaque shadows through the bevelled glass': this is a sufficient – and powerful – reminder of the danger of behaving as they are, where they are. Then, added to this is the sound of carols giving way to 'Silent Night' on a bagpipe. Here we have the innocence of carols combined with colonialism and tradition – the bagpipe – which in this context are associated with conventional expectations in general and with Katharine's husband in particular. All the messages that we could want are contained, then, in the action, the sounds, the visuals. We are witnessing an outrageous and potentially scandalous act in an ultra-conventional setting. Dialogue here would have *reduced* the effectiveness of the scene.

Beyond dramatic irony

In the short scene in the corridor we certainly have dramatic irony (this being when the audience is aware of relevant facts, whilst one or more of the characters is crucially unaware of them): we know what Almásy and Katharine have been doing, while Clifton does not, and, of course, we know that Almásy does know where Katharine is, despite his denial. Almásy is taken aback by Clifton's question partly because it comes from a Santa Claus – this could be anyone asking him; it is almost as if the question were coming from nowhere at all. But there is an added ambiguity. The exact wording of Clifton's line, 'Have you seen Katharine?' means, for Clifton, 'Do you know where Katharine is?' but his actual words must immediately remind Almásy that he has *seen* Katharine – much more fully than Clifton means – just a few seconds previously. So here we have dialogue that is not ambiguous in its intended meaning but which is received ambiguously by both the other character (Almásy) and by the audience.

In the following scene, Clifton finds Katharine and we are told in the stage directions that he 'wonders briefly how ALMÁSY had missed KATHARINE'. Of course, this stage direction is available only to readers; as audience we catch this momentary wondering on his face. Nothing is put into words. The audience is made to do a little work ('What is he thinking? Does he suspect anything?'), which involves them far more than any dialogue would. Then when he speaks, that very first word 'Darling' rams home both to Katharine and to us the nature of the situation, though Clifton would be entirely unaware of the poignancy of that word for Katharine (and us) at that moment. The lack of dialogue in the love-making scene is now contrasted with Clifton's slightly bumbling verbal ineptitude. 'You poor sausage' carries with it just that innocent, non-sensual, dated, upper-middle-class convention-ality which immediately emphasises the huge gulf in personality between this man and Almásy.

The subtle ambiguities continue. Katharine emphasises that she is hot rather than ill; we know that her being flushed at this point is not merely a result of the weather. Clifton then comments, 'Lady H said she thought you might be pregnant.' This too carries various meanings and associations. There is the literal one – Lady H's opinion – and then there is Clifton's unstated hope that Lady H might be right; Katharine, meanwhile, has the again unstated, fervent wish that she is not pregnant by Clifton, and is also instantly reminded (as are we) that she may indeed be pregnant – though as a direct result of the immediately preceding events. The great skill here is in giving Clifton lines which are entirely credible, absolutely in accordance with his character and the situation, while the same lines throw up all these nuances of meaning and association for the other character and for the audience.

When Clifton suggests taking Katharine home – meaning their house locally – she immediately re-interprets this as *home* – England; 'close to tears', she implores him to take her there, saying how desperately homesick she is. Clifton, of course, is meant to take this at face value. Katharine may not be entirely conscious of her own motivation: this, after all, is the same woman who has been in the passionate embrace of her lover just a few moments earlier. So what are we, the audience, to make of her speech? True, she may well be missing England, and she may wish she could be whisked back there – but surely not because she misses England, but rather in order to escape the position she now finds herself in. It is precisely because she wants Almásy so much that she feels this sudden desperate need to be as far from temptation as possible, as far as possible from the dilemma, the betrayal, from her own desire and what it might lead her to. Yet none of this is directly expressed. This meaning is not stated there in the words: the audience has to work to piece together the full meaning since the dialogue is operating at a level beyond the literal.

Never clearly stating the issues

This is the high point of non-literal meaning in the scene, but there are further examples in the remaining few lines. Clifton prosaically remarks that they cannot return home, as war might be declared very soon; Katherine pokes at his Santa Claus costume, with 'Oh Geoffrey, you do so love a disguise.' Certainly Clifton is wearing a disguise, but Katharine seems to be saying that Clifton really does not want to go back to England anyway, and the reason he gives is only a convenient excuse. The line may mean more than this, too. Does Clifton suspect something between Katharine and Almásy? Does he suspect something, yet not want to see it? (And does Katharine realise this?) Does he fail to respond positively to her suggestion that they should go back to England because this might force him to acknowledge the real reason for it? These questions are never fully resolved – *and are never clearly stated in the dialogue* – yet the ambiguity of this scene and a number of others certainly raises the questions in the mind of the audience, questions which linger long after the film has ended.

Of course, it is Katharine who is really wearing a disguise – that of the faithful wife, a meaning which Clifton seems to unwittingly underline: '...you do so love a disguise.' 'I do so love you.' In loving her he is loving a disguise. The fact that neither character may be conscious of this last meaning in 'I do so love you' does not diminish the fact that the dialogue carries the meaning anyway, almost despite the characters. Here, then, we have a non-literal meaning that seems to be communicated direct from scriptwriter to audience without the awareness of either of the characters, yet at the same time expressed through their lines which are entirely convincing and do not for a moment seem forced.

This 'non-stating' in the dialogue is not just a matter of clever-ness; nor, in this particular context, does it merely involve the audience further by making us work. Nor is a just a matter of reflecting more accurately how people relate to each other. Rather, the ambiguity hugely increases the *tension* in what is already a tremendously tense situation. For the characters – and for us – to finally know something, without any doubts, releases the tension. In art as in life, knowing the truth, however terrible, gnaws less at the soul than being in constant doubt. And a script that genuinely gnaws at the soul is a strong script, gripping the attention of the audience. In a script aimed at maintaining tension, elements of doubt – of ambiguity – can be extremely valuable. The dialogue must not attempt to clarify characters' motivations and knowledge but rather to hint at them. We must be left to try to fathom out the rest.

The scene ends with more straightforward dramatic irony. Clifton kisses Katharine's head and asks what she smells of. She is horrified, and so (identifying with Katharine) are we: he might guess that it is Almásy she actually smells of. But then he realises what it is: 'Marzipan! I think you've got marzipan in your hair! No wonder you're homesick.' Katharine is relieved – it is not the smell of Almásy after all – but it is only the audience that fully under-stands: ironically, this marzipan, which Clifton associates with the very English Christmas cake, *is* in fact the smell of Almásy; we have seen him picking marzipan off a piece of cake and it is this which has found its way into Katharine's hair (probably without her being conscious of it). Once again, the dialogue is made to carry ambiguities of which the characters are only partly aware.

In this example from *The English Patient*, then, we have a multitude of non-literal meanings in the dialogue. Some of the lines are clearly intending to deceive, while others are much more ambiguous, carrying a number of valid meanings simultaneously and at times allowing characters to deceive even themselves. The dialogue is never made to work too hard (in the case of the first scene quoted, it is not made to work at all!) and yet accomplishes a great deal. It is concise without ever seeming abrupt. Not a word is wasted, yet it entirely avoids any impression of artificiality. This is naturalism, yet pared to the bone; and the more spare it is, the more meanings it seems to carry.

Halls of mirrors of meanings

While much of our conversation has elements of ambiguity, sometimes it is more straightforwardly duplicitous. Mere lies, though, are of little interest in themselves. Far more arresting is the lie told with wit, the lie which at the same time in some ways may tell the truth. With this in mind, let us examine an extract from what is in most ways an utterly different type of text, Oscar Wilde's late Victorian comic classic, *The Importance of Being Earnest*. The tone of witty untruths is established at the very start of the play:

> *Morning-room in Algernon's flat in Half-Moon Street. The room is luxuriously and artistically furnished. The sound of a piano is heard in the adjoining room.*
> *(LANE is arranging afternoon tea on the table and, after the music has ceased, ALGERNON enters.)*

ALGERNON: Did you hear what I was playing, Lane?
LANE: I didn't think it polite to listen, sir.

Here we have moved immediately into the non-literal. Lane's line is both true and not true. In one sense Lane could not fail to listen: we, the audience, could hear the piano being played, so he must have too. But then that is hearing as opposed to listening. Perhaps Lane did not actively listen. So his hearing/listening statement is both true and untrue. What of the reason he gives, that he felt it would have been impolite to listen? This is surely absurd, as playing the piano is hardly private, so it must follow that what he says is untrue. At the same time, however, the line is only an exaggerated version of what was expected of servants in those times: perhaps he *did* tell himself that he ought not to listen, just as he would have refrained from listening to a private conversation. But it is more ambiguous even than this: Algernon's playing, as he goes on to admit, is not accurate ('anyone can play accurately – but I play with wonderful expression'), so Lane is pretending that he did not listen to it in order to avoid having to make a comment about it. And this pretence is absolutely in line with what is expected of a servant – that a servant should not eavesdrop on what is private – and thus places him beyond reproach. But is the pretence expected to be believed, and does Algernon in fact believe it? Here is further ambiguity. Probably the pretence is not expected to be believed and is not believed, but allows Algernon himself to comment on his own lack of pianistic accuracy – a much more acceptable procedure for him than having the servant comment on it. Yet the conversation continues as if the pretence is believed, as only then may the dignity of each be maintained. The two characters, then, willingly enter into this little charade.

The dialogue in this tiny extract is certainly self-consciously clever in a manner that is entirely absent from *The English Patient*, yet both dialogues share a richness of ambiguity. Of course, the audience, on hearing these lines, does not set about an analysis – any more than the playwright is likely to have done – but the richness of the ambiguities, and in this case their comic effects, are felt none the less strongly for that.

Wilde litters his dialogue with the unexpected. Surprises make us laugh:

JACK: My brother.
MISS PRISM: More shameful debts and extravagance?
CHASUBLE: Still leading his life of pleasure?
JACK: (*shaking his head*) Dead!
CHASUBLE: Your brother Ernest dead?
JACK: Quite dead.
MISS PRISM: What a lesson for him! I trust he will profit by it.

Certainly, Miss Prism's final comment is funny partly because it is so unexpected: it has an element of the absurd. Yet at the same time it is only an extension of her general attitude of severe disapproval of self-indulgence and the belief that we should all learn and profit from our experiences. It is as if her wish for Ernest to be punished for his wrong-doings, and for him to become a more moral character as a result, blinds her to the little inconvenience that he has actually died. Here once again we are in the world of the non-literal: she means her words to be taken literally, but we can't accept them in that way!

Let us look at a more extended example in similar vein:

LADY BRACKNELL: (*pencil and note-book in hand*) I feel bound
    to tell you that you are not down on my list of eligible young

men, although I have the same list as the dear Duchess of Bolton has. We work together, in fact. However, I am quite ready to enter your name, should your answers be what a really affectionate mother requires. Do you smoke?

JACK: Well, yes, I must admit I smoke.

LADY BRACKNELL: I am glad to hear it. A man should always have an occupation of some kind. There are too many idle men in London as it is. How old are you?

JACK: Twenty-nine.

LADY BRACKNELL: A very good age to be married at. I have always been of the opinion that a man who desires to get married should know everything or nothing. Which do you know?

JACK: (*after some hesitation*) I know nothing, Lady Bracknell.

LADY BRACKNELL: I am pleased to hear it. I do not approve of anything that tampers with natural ignorance. Ignorance is like a delicate exotic fruit; touch it and the bloom is gone. The whole theory of modern education is radically unsound. Fortunately in England, at any rate, education produces no effect whatsoever. If it did, it would prove a serious danger to the upper classes, and probably lead to acts of violence in Grosvenor Square.

Here we have dialogue which deliciously mixes the true with the absurd. Again, there is much of the unexpected, a number of statements being florid embellishments of precisely the opposite of what one might reasonably anticipate. Lady Bracknell lauds ignorance rather than education and praises smoking as though it were a serious occupation. Yet merely to have a character present the reverse of that which is normally expressed would be tedious: what makes these arresting – and amusing – is that these statements do have their roots in real life, real experience. They are a mixture of gross exaggeration and truths which are expressed with a shocking honesty.

Lady Bracknell's first speech in this extract may be a parody of upper-class attitudes of the time, but we can almost believe that she *would* work together with some other dowager. Her use of the word 'affectionate' is particularly choice, since it contains an element of ambiguity. Surely no truly affectionate mother would be so calculating, but on the other hand, perhaps this is how such people genuinely show affection. (We will recognise this ambiguity – and be all the more amused by it – if, as is invariably the case with this play, the part is played straight. In this way, the actress implies that there is no question but that Lady Bracknell believes every word she says, so leaving the audience to do much of the work.) The lines about smoking, too, seem absurd, but at the same time amuse us because they remind us of how pointless, unchallenging and trifling the lives of many of the upper classes are.

The final paragraph of this extract is a little more complex. Lady Bracknell's opinions may at first appear ridiculous, though they are based on an attitude which does exist. But when she goes on to say that fortunately in England, education is completely ineffectual, she is making a point which is much closer to reality (though the *attitude* – the 'fortunately' – is what is different) – since she is surely absolutely right that if education really were effective it would, or at least ought to, 'prove a serious danger to the upper classes'. Here, then, is dialogue which surprisingly mixes wildly exaggerated attitudes with truths that are approached from an unorthodox direction. It is this mix which keeps us on our toes, by playing with our expectations. *The Importance of Being Earnest*, like the previous, utterly different example, thus succeeds in *using dialogue to reflect the complexities of character and relationships, rather than producing simplifications of them.*

Consistency of style

It might be objected that this type of dialogue is artificial. Of course it is artificial. It is not intended to be anything else – though to be most effective it should be delivered as though it were the most normal mode of speech in the world. Wilde is not pretending that this is how people really speak to each other, but nevertheless it does bear some relation to the effete upper-class speech of the period. Wilde is indulging his love of word-play at the same time as parodying the style of speech, as well as the attitudes, of this class of people. But we don't listen to it as though we were listening to the dialogue of *The English Patient* or any number of other scripts which deal in heightened naturalism – if we do, we will soon become very irritated. We listen to it for what it is, with its own limitations but with its own delights.

This leads us on to a major consideration for the writer of

dialogue: consistency of style. Any script represents a certain world, in which certain sorts of things happen. These worlds vary from writer to writer, and in many cases from script to script within the output of each writer. *A Midsummer Night's Dream*, for example, inhabits a magical, innocent world, where there may be misunderstandings but there is little real malice. *Othello*, on the other hand, inhabits a world of worldly cynicism and deceit, where no fairies may be expected to come to the aid of anyone. Indeed, if fairies were suddenly to appear to Othello and make clear to him the evil of Iago and the error of his ways, we would find it totally unconvincing: the world that has been established here has no room for fairies. Similarly, in a number of Dennis Potter's television series the characters, otherwise quite naturalistically portrayed, suddenly burst into mimed song-and-dance routines. This works splendidly, as it is consistently applied; but if just one such routine were to be dropped into, say, a gritty television play by Trevor Griffiths, we simply would not accept it.

So, consistency of action is required. Consistency is also required of dialogue. As we have already seen, dialogue is not simply realistic or unrealistic, like real life or unlike real life; rather, any script is written in a particular style, a particular blend, and that blend has to be consistent within that particular script.

Dialogue as a world view

A style of dialogue represents, in effect, a world view. To shift from one style to another within the same piece can be not only disorientating; it can lead the audience to feel that the writer has lost faith in that world view. The audience itself then loses faith in the writer, the characters and the whole production. There has to be an overall consistency of tone in the dialogue. That does not mean, of course, that there cannot be light and shade – the Four Weddings needed the Funeral as well – but there must be an *overall* tone: hardly ever can a script be all things to everyone.

A consistency of tone in dialogue has less to do with lightness or seriousness than it has to do with *the position of the script in relation to naturalism*. After all, there are many serious scripts which are also funny, and many essentially comic pieces which have their serious moments; very often these contrasts enhance the effectiveness of the rest of the script. But if a script is written with the dialogue at a certain distance from naturalism, or as presenting itself as simply naturalistic, then a departure from this tone will be difficult to carry off. In a Dario Fo political farce, for example, we know that the dialogue is funny and biting; it is satirical in tone. A section of straight, naturalistic dialogue inserted into it, however well it might accord with the meaning of the play (the section might be about some aspect of corruption, say), would nevertheless feel inappropriate. Not only would we probably not be able to accept it, but it also might mar our enjoyment of the rest of the production as well. The tone of dialogue in a script is something a writer may well not decide upon before starting to write, but it will soon emerge as the script takes shape, and as it does so it must be recognised and respected. Taking liberties with the tone of dialogue within a script is a dangerous business.

Let us complete this chapter by looking at an extract from the celebrated film *Pulp Fiction* (writers, Quentin Tarantino and Roger Avary). In this script the writers' control of tone is wonderful, though it is that very control of tone which mixes the hilarious with the horrific that is particularly shocking; it seems to imply an almost complete lack of moral framework. It is not so much the violence that shocks as the attitudes towards it, or – if such a concept can exist – the *lack* of attitudes towards it. We will see something comparable but rather different when we turn to *Goodfellas* (actually a highly moral film). *Pulp Fiction* also makes tremendously effective use of time. It is almost commonplace now for a film to start at a certain point in the action, jump backwards, catch up with itself and then move on to the end; *Pulp Fiction*, though, manages to finish in the middle, in terms of time, while at least one of the main characters – whom we have already seen killed – is still very much alive. In a variety of ways, then, the script is innovative. This applies to Tarantino's dialogue just as much as to every other element of his film-making. From his youth, Tarantino soaked himself in film, and certainly there are clear influences in his work of earlier gangster movies, but never before had there been dialogue quite like that which he and Avary create in *Pulp Fiction*. In the following extract Vincent and Jules are chatting away, driving down the streets of Hollywood:

VINCENT
...But you know what the funniest thing about Europe is?

JULES

What?

VINCENT

It's the little differences. I mean, they got the same shit over there that we got here, but it's just, there it's a little different.

JULES

Example?

VINCENT

Well, you can walk into a movie theatre and buy a beer. And I don't mean just, like, in no paper cup. I'm talking about a glass of beer. And in Paris, you can buy a beer at McDonald's. And, you know what they call a Quarter-Pounder with Cheese in Paris?

JULES

They don't call it a Quarter-Pounder with Cheese?

VINCENT

No, man, they got the metric system there, they wouldn't know what the fuck a Quarter-Pounder is.

JULES

What'd they call it?

VINCENT

They call it a Royale with Cheese.

JULES

(*repeating*)
Royale with Cheese.

VINCENT

Yeah, that's right.

JULES

What'd they call a Big Mac?

VINCENT
Well, Big Mac's a Big Mac, but they call it Le Big Mac.

JULES
Le Big Mac. What do they call a Whopper?

VINCENT
I dunno, I didn't go into a Burger King. But you know what they put on French fries in Holland instead of ketchup?

JULES
What?

VINCENT
Mayonnaise.

JULES
Goddam!

VINCENT
I seen 'em do it, man. They fuckin' drown 'em in that shit.

JULES
Yuck!

This, of course, is all pretty daft. Despite the casual expletives it is also quite charming and amusing. But its full significance only becomes apparent as the sequence continues. The dialogue immediately following this, as they get out of the car and walk towards an apartment building, is conducted in the same relaxed, almost throw-away manner, such that we have to do a double-take to realise that they are in fact agreeing that for this sort of job, with three or four men upstairs, they really ought to have been issued with shotguns. As they make their way through the courtyard and then on up through the apartment building the chat reverts to lighter matters again – how their boss met his girlfriend, what she does for a living and what the boss does to people he suspects might be getting too close to her. They finally reach their destination, but, realising that they are a few minutes early, they stand outside the door continuing their chit-chat – *which they are actually taking quite seriously*; this conversation is of real interest to them, and whatever they are about to do occupies their minds very little. But while waiting in the corridor they do lower their voices a little, almost as if they were in some sort of waiting room and are not wanting to disturb anyone. Finally they enter the room, and soon they have shot all the men in there.

The extract quoted above, then, takes on a completely new meaning in retrospect. What at first appears to be merely the idle chatter of two engaging young men has to be completely re-assessed – these men are talking in this manner while they are on their way to perform an execution. Even during the one interlude where they actually address the matter in hand – the adequacy or otherwise of their firearms for the job – there is no real tension in the dialogue, just a little mild irritation with their superiors, just as any office worker might express a mild annoyance about the inefficiency of some other administrators. Right up to the very point of entering the room the dialogue continues in the same vein.

This is dialogue which is about what it appears to be about – trivia, though taken fairly seriously – for the characters speaking, but is about much more for the audience. This dialogue – not because of what it *is* about, but precisely because of what it is *not* about – tells us a great deal about Jules and Vincent: their attitude towards their work and their priorities. Vincent registers shock – 'Goddam...Yuck' – at the idea of mayonnaise on French fries but clearly feels no such strong emotions at the prospect of gunning a few people down. This dialogue is a great deal more effective in displaying how these characters tick than any speeches directly about the subject would be.

During the scene of the shootings in the apartment-rooms the dialogue returns for a while – almost surrealistically – to the subject of burgers and their French names, but what had been an innocent passing of the time of day now becomes a subject of something like interrogation for the occupants. It is like a nightmare based upon reality (reality was the previous treatment of this topic; now we have the nightmare); the dialogue here is a frightening display of Jules's arbitrary wielding of power. He treats this utterly irrelevant subject as one which is as good as any to humiliate these people. Now, dialogue which earlier had seemed pointless but amusing takes on a completely different and terrifying complexion in this reworking.

So what might we gain from all this? First we learn the tremendous power of dialogue which is about something quite other than the subject that ought to be uppermost in the minds of the characters (in a very different context, Pinter also uses this technique to great effect), rather displaying *state of mind* and *attitude*, however unwittingly on the part of the characters. Second, we learn the effectiveness of returning to previous subjects – however irrelevant they may seem – and reworking them in a new context (which, by coincidence or not, is also a favourite technique of Pinter's). In musical terms this is rather like taking a melody and transforming it into another, quite different melody, as composers from Bach to Richard Strauss to Andrew Lloyd Weber have done. There is always something strangely arresting about returning to a melody but finding that it has been turned into some completely new entity; at an unconscious level it is as if we were being shown what any one thing in life may lead to, what it may be transformed into. The experience may be frightening or not; it is certainly engaging. It is not easy to make this work in dialogue, but it is possible.

One word of caution: this dialogue style has many imitators, and there are others who, if not exactly imitators, have anyway been working along similar lines. In *Amateur*, for example, Hal Hartley presents us with a number of scenes in which the dialogue acts very much as it does in *Pulp Fiction*; at one point we are with two hit-men who have just committed a murder. One is hungry and says he's going to get a couple of take-aways. The other tells him to remember to get a receipt. This request to get a receipt could certainly be a line from *Pulp Fiction*: they may be hit-men but they are also workers; they are doing their job and the take-away is a legitimate expense, so they should remember the receipt. But in the context of the murder they have just committed this line is shocking, displaying as in *Pulp Fiction* the attitudes and priorities of the characters. *Amateur* was certainly not in any way a copy of *Pulp Fiction* (the two were released in the same year) but it could be in danger of seeming so. There is peril for us scriptwriters in writing a style of dialogue which is too clearly identified with a particular writer; the work of Tarantino is extremely distinctive, so poor imitations are usually easy to spot. Rather than imitate, we should try to learn the lessons and then apply them in our own, personal way.

6. Heightened Naturalism

The convention established by the script

We have already examined naturalism in dialogue, and in Chapter 5 noted the need for consistency of style. Now we move on to look at some of the ways in which naturalism may be heightened, and combine this with a closer look at consistency of style in the context of that heightened naturalism.

So, *what is heightened naturalism?*

There are some styles of dialogue which are very obviously not naturalistic. Often, indeed, they draw attention to this. Just to limit ourselves to the theatre for the moment, the list would include writers as varied as Brecht, Beckett, Pinter, Dylan Thomas, Edward Bond, Tony Harrison and Derek Walcott, while from a much earlier period we might call up such names as Shakespeare, Jonson or Webster. These are all writers from whom we can learn: they each create highly stylised dialogue, which we will examine in a later chapter. But in this chapter we are looking at a different style of writing, used by writers such as Shaw, Arthur Miller, Tennessee Williams, Tom Stoppard, David Hare, Athol Fugard, Caryl Churchill, David Mamet, Sam Shepard and April de Angelis. These are writers who have inherited the essentially naturalistic mantle of Chekhov and Ibsen, but have not always been content to leave dialogue as being closely imitative of speech in 'real life': they have taken it beyond naturalism. However, unlike those others named above, they do not positively draw attention to their artifice. Their writing is in a style I shall call *heightened naturalism*, and we can learn from them, too.

Of course, the distinction between these two types of writers is itself an artificial one, and many scriptwriters do not sit happily in either category. Stoppard, for example, at times seems firmly in the naturalistic camp, while at other times is a clear inheritor of the tradition of Beckett (Stoppard's Rosencrantz and Guildenstern bear an obvious family resemblance to Beckett's Estragon and Vladimir in *Waiting for Godot*); a great deal of Pinter's early work falls clearly into the non-naturalistic category, while much of his later work is closer to heightened naturalism; in some of her scripts, such as *Blue Heart*, Caryl Churchill is extravagantly non-naturalistic, while a play such as *Serious Money* inhabits the world of heightened naturalism. Yet, however many writers straddle the categories, I do think the general division is useful for scriptwriters to bear in mind. On the one hand there are the scripts which invite the audience to recognise the hand of the writer, the art of the production; while on the other hand there are the scripts in which the hand of the writer is kept fairly consistently concealed, but in which the naturalism of dialogue is in some way heightened.

As scriptwriters we have a choice. We do not simply write whatever dialogue comes to mind: we can choose the style in which that dialogue is to be written. For the dialogue to work well, that choice needs to be an informed and conscious one. What is important is not, ultimately, whether the dialogue in a script is written naturalistically or not. What is important is that it should be convincing: this means that within the convention of dialogue *that the script has itself established*, it must feel natural. The intoxicating dialogue of David Mamet's magnificent *Glengarry Glen Ross*, for example, can really be found nowhere else, but we accept it not so much because we think it is real as because it is consistent. Here we have a writer who imitates every tiny nuance of speech – every ungrammatical sentence, every false start, interruption, repetition – and then *heightens* this naturalism to a point of almost ghastly poetry. But it is at one with itself, so we accept it.

Yet consistency of style in itself allows a writer to produce some *inconsistency* of style! A Tom Stoppard or an Arthur Miller, a Trevor Griffiths or an Alan Bleasdale – they all appear to present naturalistic dialogue, yet in fact each of them presents their own particular brand of dialogue. (Their styles may overlap, yet we would surely immediately distinguish, say, a page of Stoppard from a page of Bleasedale.) Each of them gains our trust by their consistency of style, and is then in a position gently to move us a little closer to poetry, and to take us with them. For example, near the end of Griffiths' *Comedians*, Price – one of the trainee comics – turns his ire full on Waters, his supposed teacher. But the speech is not just an outpouring of anger or bitterness, nor merely an accusation that Waters has sold out: it is also a sort of impassioned poetry. And we accept it. It is only pushing a little further the style that Griffiths has already had us accept. Or in the Requiem at the end of Miller's *Death of a Salesman* we can witness Charley, that most prosaic of onlookers, speaking words of rare beauty. In part, as in the previous example, we can accept this given the strength of feeling on the occasion (as pointed out in Chapter 1, strength of feeling does often lead to highly rhythmic and sometimes poetic use of language in normal life), but it is not just this: we accept it as an extension of the language already present in the script.

The following is an extract from a television play of my own, *No Further Cause for Concern*. Danny is one of a number of prisoners holding Green, a Prison Officer, hostage. Danny and the others are compiling a list of demands to present to the Governor:

DANNY: All right, correspondence. Now read that back.

ALEC: Enquiry. Brutality, visits, association, exercise, workshops, correspondence.

DANNY: And food while we're at it.

GREEN: You want Butlins don't you.

DANNY: No we don't want soddin' Butlins, but being in prison is the punishment –

GREEN: I know that.

DANNY: We're not sent here to be punished, we're sent here as punishment. Loss of liberty, that's the punishment. Loss of walking down the street, loss of going for a pint, loss of being able to screw, having to put up with doing it with other poor sods like him (WALLY) to stop yourself from going mad. Loss of your time. It's not your time now, it's theirs. All right so the great British public couldn't give a shit what happens to us, makes 'em feel better if they know we're being clobbered, shows how much more they're worth than we are, all right, but that's not what the law says. Giving up your freedom, that's the punishment, not being treated like bloody animals.

GREEN: And that's what you think we do.

DANNY: Think?

GREEN: We just carry out orders. And we're as pleasant as you lot'll let us be.

DANNY: And you was ordered to beat up Phil Kitchen.

GREEN: I didn't, and you know it.

DANNY: Your lot did.

GREEN: But not me. Isn't it what you always complain about, being accused of things other people have done? All being tarred with the same brush?

DANNY: Oh, sod the lot of you!

Here again we have a highly charged atmosphere, which allows us to accept the more readily the eloquence of Danny. And the scriptwriter must aim for eloquence at times, must at times aim for beauty. There are risks, however. In this speech ('We're not sent here... ') I have never been entirely sure whether I had led the audience to suspend their disbelief sufficiently, or whether – despite the response of Green, the Prison Officer, presenting the other side of the argument – the dialogue here comes across as too preachy, and in a language not quite credible for this character. Of course, these risks may be run without any heightening of the naturalism at all. We can have a character preaching to the audience (and, generally, losing their sympathy) without straying from the most humdrum realism – this happens in many plays but also, in a different form, in many soap operas – and matching character to speech pattern can also be problematic in any style. However, these do appear to be particularly strong risks when the naturalism is heightened – when we know we are stretching the stylistic conventions of dialogue which we have already established in any given script.

A scriptwriter's world

In the context of consistency of style of dialogue, it seems appropriate here to say a word about the limits of that style for any one scriptwriter. Some writers feel entirely comfortable moving from one type of social world to another, but for many the particular voice which we associate with their dialogue is only in part a matter of style itself – it is more a matter of the clearly delineated world which they tend to inhabit. Ayckbourn is most comfortable with the middle classes, for example, while John Godber is most at home with the rough-and-tumble end of working-class life. Stoppard is almost always at his best when presenting the intelligentsia (indeed, the dialogue given to the one working-class character to appear in his play *The Real Thing* is almost embarrassing).

What are the dangers of a scriptwriter limiting the spread of types of characters? One danger is simply that the world presented may feel too small – as audience we may want to break out of the confines imposed upon us. If we watch a production full of the well-off middle classes nattering about second cars and second homes we may soon start to itch to have a labourer burst in, and vice-versa. But it is not only that the world presented may seem too narrow; a further danger is that too many of the characters may begin to sound very much like each other.

There are two extremes here, both of which are to be avoided. One extreme is to fill a script with people who sound (and probably look and act) as different from each other as possible. In this type of script, every character speaks in an obviously distinctive way, each with distinct regional (or, even better, national) accents, and clear marks of class, education, occupation, etc. However interesting the contrasts between the characters may be, though, this approach smacks too much of, 'Once upon a time there was an Englishman, an Irishman and a Scotsman...' It is the scriptwriter's version of social engineering, and feels artificial. It does, though, at least have the benefit of allowing the writer relatively easily to produce dialogue in which the speech of each character is clearly differentiated from that of the next.

The other extreme is to create a set of characters all of whom come from the same class and probably from the same area, and have the same types of jobs. Here the writer is more likely to be able to present an image of how a community or sub-group functions, and the contrasts between the attitudes of characters, although less obvious than at the other extreme, might well benefit from being more subtle. The great danger with this approach, however, has already been noted: the characters may use language in ways which are too similar to each other.

So the writer has a choice. Writing within a smaller range, while at first sight easier, is in fact very difficult in terms of dialogue: it is harder to differentiate the language of characters when they come from very similar backgrounds. Having your script peopled with characters from a wide range of backgrounds, on the other hand, can not only look artificial but also brings other difficulties, as the writer must have a genuine knowledge of how all these types of individuals might speak.

So, how far should we limit ourselves in the scope of the 'dialogue world' which we create in a script? My own opinion is that we should stretch ourselves as far as we feel confident – and no further! This means that we should listen as carefully as possible to the speech of all those with whom we come into contact, to try to make use of it, but we should never try to imitate a style of speech with which we are not genuinely familiar (unless in obvious parody – and even this is risky). Some writers have had the good fortune to mix in very varied circles and thus to have learned first-hand the speech patterns of various social groupings – by class, geography, gender, occupation, etc. as outlined in Chapter 1 – but most have not had this breadth of experience. Ultimately, better the Wesker or the Wilde who sticks to the world they know than the scriptwriter who ventures all over the dialogue universe but convinces no-one.

We should try to avoid scattering people from very varied backgrounds through a script just for the sake of different types of voices and speech patterns. The background (and thus style of speech) of each character should be chosen for different reasons, to do not only with plot but also with each character's role in the *meaning* of the piece. Characters may be created and developed around the contrasts with each other *as characters*, but never merely to make the life of the scriptwriter easier in terms of differentiating dialogue. (The only exception to this is in parts which are very minor indeed, where there is very little rounded characterisation and one may as well vary the speech patterns.)

Naturalism in non-naturalism

There are times when a scriptwriter may choose to alter the effect of dialogue not so much by the words themselves, as by how he or she chooses to present them. So a section of dialogue which is in essence naturalistic may be heightened by being presented in a way which is not naturalistic. The words may be 'normal', but the context is not.

Let me give some very different examples of this. The first technique is a very common one; the particular example comes from the film *French Kiss*. Here, the two central characters are deep in conversation, walking through Paris; they reach a park bench, where they continue talking. We see them first walking in the street and then – obviously a minute or two later – seated on the park bench, yet there is no break in the conversation at all. Here we are not shown two snippets of a conversation, but rather are presented with one continuous piece of dialogue despite the fact that there is a jump of time and place in the middle of it. On the one hand the writer has wanted to avoid a break in the flow of speech and thought, and yet on the other he has wanted to imply that the conversation took place over a lengthy stretch of time. So he has it both ways, and in effect stretches reality a little. We are not meant to notice the impossibility of what we see and hear: it is a sleight of hand (Shakespeare frequently employs similar sleights of hand, particularly through use of two simultaneous and ultimately contradictory time-schemes). This is a non-naturalism that has no wish to be seen as such, so the effect is really one of heightened naturalism rather than of conspicuous artifice.

The second example makes no attempt at concealing its art. In the film *Ocean's 11* (writers, Ted Griffin and Steven Soderbergh) there is a sequence held together by a continuous piece of dialogue, in which one of the thieves asks another whether they can possibly succeed in all the tasks necessary to rob the casino. At the same time, across the conversation, what we actually see is those tasks being tackled: it is not clear at that moment whether we are seeing the reality – jumping into the future – or one of the character's vision of what might be possible. Either way, while the dialogue (and incidentally, the action itself) is naturalistic, its *presentation* is not. Similarly, towards the end of the film, we only see the robbery itself after the event has taken place. This is not a conventional 'flashback', just as the earlier example was not a 'flash forward', in the sense of being sustained scenes; rather, they are illustrations of the story-telling within the dialogue at each point. The playing with time and place is all in the context of the naturalism of the speeches.

A third example comes from Alan Ayckbourn, whose work has changed in many ways over the years. In his earlier plays such as *Bedroom Farce* or *The Norman Conquests*, Ayckbourn set out to explore individuals' social and particularly sexual weaknesses, and although his primary aim appears to have been to amuse, there always seems to have been a conscience lurking somewhere in the dialogue. By the mid-eighties, though, his priorities had changed. His plays were (and still are) funny, but the moral tone had become more pronounced. Yet his technique, though having been refined over the years, had not in essence altered. The actual language is close to naturalism (of course selected, edited, chopped around, a little exaggerated here and there), yet the speeches are often very funny, above all because of the situations people find themselves in. But Ayckbourn sometimes adds a further element which heightens the effect of the naturalistic dialogue: he so constructs many of the scenes as to allow us to witness more than one scene taking place at the same time. In one of his earlier plays he allows us to witness two dinner parties simultaneously – the lines spin off each other, providing not only dramatic irony but continually adding new meanings in addition to those intended by the speakers. By the eighties, and now at the National Theatre, he has a bigger budget to play with, so in *A Small Family Business* he presents us with a set which is a cross-section of a complete house – kitchen, double living-room, bedrooms, bathroom, the lot. There are some wonderful sequences where events are taking place *simultaneously* in a number of these places. The effect is not only of tremendous vitality and life, but also of lines from separate locations appearing to have an effect on each other. It allows, too, for the dialogue in the different places to be in completely different moods, which also can then play off each other. This is an extreme example, but there are many others less extreme (and more affordable!) of simultaneous scenes adding new levels of meaning to dialogue.

The final example of apparently naturalistic dialogue presented in a non-naturalistic manner comes from the work of Woody Allen. Allen's dialogue is superb. Some complain that it is limited in scope and even that it is repetitive in tone (both of which can apply to many successful writers), but the dialogue is, nevertheless, excellent. In what way? He catches quite wonderfully all that messiness of language referred to in Chapter 1, usually transforming it for comic effect. Some writers produce very funny scripts which rely mainly on jokes; there are some scripts which rely heavily on situation (such as Ayckbourn's); and there are others in which the humour arises directly out of the characters. Woody Allen's work falls into this last category. Of course, there are jokes and there are situations which set up the humour, but nevertheless the humour in Allen's dialogue is created primarily from his accurate depiction of character. Very often there is an element of the pathetic in Allen's leading characters: they spend much of their time trying to explain themselves, convince themselves, justify themselves or raise their own status (by however tiny a degree), so that we laugh at them but at the same time as we laugh with them. They are weak but warmly drawn, so we allow ourselves to recognise ourselves in them.

The dialogue itself, though, is really a very clever, subtle form of naturalism. It is frequently sophisticated in terms of meaning, and certainly is frequently subtle in variations of tone, yet it feels almost as though it has been improvised. Often, though, Allen will use the *form* in which he presents the dialogue to further heighten its effect. In the following example, from near the start of *Annie Hall*, the main character, Alvy, has up to this point been narrating as an adult voice-over. The scene takes place in a classroom, where we have just seen the child Alvy kiss 1st Girl:

1st GIRL: (*Making noises*) Ugh, he kissed me, he kissed me.
TEACHER: (*Offscreen*) That's the second time this month! Step up here!
    As the teacher, really glaring now, speaks, Alvy rises from his seat and moves over to her. Angry, she points with her hand while the students turn their heads to watch what will happen next.
ALVY: What'd I do?
TEACHER: Step up here.
ALVY: What'd I do?
TEACHER: You should be ashamed of yourself.
    The students, their heads still turned, look back at Alvy, now an adult, sitting in the last seat of the second row.
ALVY (AS ADULT): (*First offscreen, then onscreen as camera moves over to the back of the classroom*) Why, I was just expressing a healthy sexual curiosity.
TEACHER: (*The younger Alvy standing next to her*) Six-year-old boys don't have girls on their minds.
ALVY (AS ADULT): (*Still sitting in the back of the classroom*) I did.
    The girl the young Alvy kissed turns to the older Alvy; she gestures and speaks.
1st GIRL: For God's sake, Alvy, even Freud speaks of a latency period.
ALVY (AS ADULT): (*Gesturing*) Well, I never had a latency period. I can't help it.
TEACHER: (*With young Alvy still at her side*) Why couldn't you have been more like Donald? (*The camera pans over to Donald, sitting up tall in his seat, then back to the teacher*) Now, there was a model boy!
ALVY (AS CHILD): (*Still standing next to the teacher*) Tell the folks where you are today, Donald.

DONALD: I run a profitable dress company.
ALVY'S VOICE: Right. Sometimes I wonder where my classmates
are today.
*The camera shows the full classroom, the students sitting
behind their desks, the teacher standing in front of the room.
One at a time, the young students rise up from their desks
and speak.*
1st BOY: I'm President of the Pinkus Plumbing Company.
2nd BOY: I sell tallises.
3rd BOY: I used to be a heroin addict. Now I'm a methadone
addict.
2nd GIRL: I'm into leather.

For much of this extract Allen is not producing dialogue which is
'non-naturalistic' in the sense of speech which is highly poetic, or
which is in a style in which no-one would normally speak. Rather,
he is heightening the effect of the dialogue by presenting it in an
almost surreal way. As the scene progresses, however, the line
between heightened naturalism and non-naturalism becomes
blurred. Allen is not content to have one of his characters act as
both narrator and younger self – he has to have the other characters actually interact with the older narrator, whom now we not
only hear but also see. Part of the delight of this arises from Allen's
playing with the conventions of narration (this will be discussed
further in a later chapter). The words spoken may be fairly
ordinary but the context becomes so extraordinary that we start to
question everything – the surrealism is really limited to the presentation but it feels as if it has infected the dialogue itself. The added
fun here comes from putting the dialogue of adults into the mouths
of children. The open manipulation, the playful display of the hand
of the author, is certainly non-naturalistic. Here, then, the
scriptwriter is straddling the line between naturalism and non-
naturalism, basically using the former in terms of the actual words
used, but the latter in the form in which they are presented, thus
creating extremely arresting effects of which dialogue forms a part.

7. Tone, Pace and Conflict

Light and shade

If consistency of dialogue style is vital for a successful script, being a major element in establishing the convention that the particular script creates, then attention to *tone* and *pace* in the dialogue is equally important, as they contribute to the production of light and shade within that overall consistency of dialogue. We must also look at how these elements are tied into both the climaxes and meanings within the script.

Consistency of dialogue style is, as we have already seen, essentially about the relationship with naturalism in the dialogue. Tone is different. Tone may be ironic, light, serious or tragic, and it may be any of these in whatever style of dialogue has been adopted, at whatever distance from naturalism the scriptwriter may choose. Tone, then, should not be confused with style, though the two do certainly affect each other (and it has to be admitted that it is sometimes very hard to disentangle them). Words which are close – though not identical – in meaning to 'tone', as it used here, would be 'mood' and 'atmosphere'.

One further clarification: a script will have an overall tone (perhaps one of those suggested above, or something quite different) but tone will also vary – must also vary – between one scene and another. If the tone does not vary sufficiently, the script starts to take on a monochrome quality; this can have a certain attraction but is much more likely eventually to bore the audience. Tone must be varied, and above all tone in dialogue must be varied.

It is important to establish the overall tone at the start of the script. To take one example, in *Goodfellas* we are immediately thrown into a scene which becomes appallingly violent. But the scene is not only a presentation of violence; it is also about attitudes towards violence – attitudes which are revealed in the dialogue. Three men, Jimmy, Tommy and Henry, are driving along a freeway at night. They hear a thumping noise, and react with a collection of lines full of repetition, half-listening-to-each-other responses and hesitations, annoyed by the noise and wondering whether they have a flat tyre. They stop the car and open the boot, and we see a body covered in tablecloths, soaked in blood. The body – Billy Batts – is still alive, moving. Batts manages to plead for his life, but one of the three, Tommy, is clearly angry that Batts has not died yet, and, swearing at him for being alive and yelling at him to look him in the eye while he does it, stabs him again and again while Batts squirms in the boot. For good measure Jimmy then pumps a number of bullets into the now inert body. We hear a voice-over, from Henry, telling us that from a very young age he had always wanted to be a gangster.

This opening scene is shocking, and sets the tone for the rest of the film. Certainly it establishes the tone of violence – this is in the action – but the dialogue does more than that. At the start, when they hear the thumping, the three men do actually realise that the noise is coming from the boot, and that Batts is still alive. However, we don't realise that they know until, when they get out, they go straight round to the boot and Tommy takes out a knife. What the opening dialogue gives us is a confused and exasperated conversation about whether or not they have a flat tyre – we see that they are genuinely irritated and annoyed, but at same time we come to realise that this opening conversation is in fact a sort of macabre joke: Batts is of so little importance to them that they speak about him as they would some sort of mechanical fault – he is beneath being mentioned as a human being, let alone being treated as an object of compassion.

So the dialogue establishes at the start that these people talk in a way which distances them from the meaning of violence and from suffering. It is de-humanising dialogue, at the opening of a film which will trace the de-humanising effects of gangster life. But there are two further important elements as well. The dialogue raises the issue of a particular kind of respect, Tommy yelling at Batts to look him in the eye while he stabs him to death; it is only later that we discover that Batts was all but killed in the first place for failing to be respectful to Tommy in a bar. More importantly, the dialogue establishes a tone of camaraderie: the men in the car are *together*, and talk in that highly informal, only half-listening and yet co-operative manner which sets the tone for much of the rest of the film, for *Goodfellas* is also the story of one man who is willing to do almost anything to be accepted – to be one of the 'goodfellas'.

At the start of *Goodfellas*, then, the tone of the whole film is set together with the tone of the dialogue too (and we very soon realise that Scorsese and Pileggi have leapt forwards in time in order to use these opening scenes for this purpose). This dialogue tone is bound up with the themes and meanings of the film: it is very hard to disentangle the two – dialogue tone on the one hand, themes or meanings on the other – and perhaps one should not try too hard to separate them anyway. The scriptwriter must allow the two to feed each other.

Let us look at another, very different opening, which also establishes a tone of dialogue. At the start of the film *The Player* (writer, Michael Tolkin) we are given one tracking shot of quite extraordinary length, in the car park and offices of a Hollywood studio. We move seamlessly from one conversation to another as we move through the premises. The impression is not so much of being in a single scene as of *overhearing* snatches of conversation – we feel like outsiders, eavesdroppers, at one point hearing a discussion about a film proposal from outside the office where it is taking place, through the window. In terms of shot (and precision of co-ordination in the production), then, this opening scene shows tremendous professionalism and confidence. And what of the dialogue? There is a series of speeches in which people are openly attempting to impress each other – and succeeding or otherwise – and all the dialogue is soaked in a consciousness of cinema: at one point a character mentions another film and the extraordinary length of the opening tracking shot. This is the tone of the dialogue, then – confident, smooth, cool, powerful. Again we have the establishment of a tone of dialogue which chimes in perfectly with the themes and meanings of the film. *The Player* is about the confidence, professionalism and power of film producers, and it is also about an outsider (like an eavesdropper) who has never been able to get in. We will eventually see that the plot is circular and is *about itself*; the dialogue at the start slips in this idea of referring to itself when the comment is made about another film with an exceptionally long opening tracking shot. The manner of presentation of the dialogue at the start of *The Player*, then, sets up the outsider theme, while its tone underlines the theme of the power of producers.

What we hear and what we don't

In the opening of *The Player*, the dialogue serves almost entirely to establish tone: its main function is not to assist plot or even characterisation (though it does achieve this as well), but rather to *present dialogue as a particular sort of wallpaper*, which tells a lot about the occupants who choose to live in this environment. Focusing in on a particular conversation is less important than the tone of the conversations in general.

Talking of dialogue as wallpaper, this seems an appropriate point to digress briefly on selecting what dialogue we hear as an audience and what we don't. This can be important both in plot terms and also in terms of empathy – whom we are invited to sympathise with.

Let us imagine a party, in real life. There are perhaps sixty or seventy guests. As we walk round we will hear snatches of speech from a dozen conversations. We will stop and take part in some discussions, possibly overhear a few other bits and ignore the rest. Alternatively we might take part in only one conversation all night, or we might sit in a corner close to a stereo speaker and a bowl of peanuts and say nothing to anyone. But whatever we do, the party is still there, there is still all this dialogue happening.

Now let us imagine writing a scene, or a series of scenes, set at a party. There is all this dialogue going on (except, of course, that as this isn't a party in real life there is no dialogue going on at all until we write it): which parts of it do we commit to the page?

There are a number of considerations here: the scriptwriter may choose to present (or perhaps to select) certain conversations in order to develop particular aspects of characterisation; he or she might choose to show certain speeches in order to push the plot along. But there is also the matter of empathy. When we hear dialogue it is as if we were there, listening and looking, *often over someone's shoulder*. And just our being there, at that person's shoulder, leads us to start to empathise with that character, to see the world from that character's point of view.

So, to return to the party, let's say that as the scriptwriter you want to present a major discussion about social welfare, since the inadequacy or otherwise of social provision is one of the themes in your script. How much of the discussion do we – the audience – hear? The obvious answer is: all of it. All the other conversations at the party continue to take place, of course, but we concentrate on this important debate – this is what is scripted while the rest is left to improvisation. This gives due weight to the issues and to the characters involved in the conversation. On the other hand, we may not hear all of it. We might join the party *with* a certain character – let's call her Sarah – who then hears a number of snatches of other conversations before having her interest taken by this one. This reduces the amount of dialogue shown from this particular debate (perhaps – remember that you are in control of what is said!), but adds to our empathising with Sarah: we are joining this conversation because she is (it feels as if *we* are) choosing to do so in preference to joining some other discussion, which is in itself a statement about Sarah.

Or perhaps we don't join this conversation with Sarah. Perhaps we join it with Dan, who then becomes bored with it and leaves – so we do too. This, too, makes a statement about Dan; and since there is a tendency for the audience to empathise with the character through whom we are seeing the world (the character we are 'with'), there will be a certain tendency for us to accept that character's views – in this case, that the conversation about social provision is of limited interest – more readily than we might otherwise. (To revert for a moment to *Goodfellas*, if we were not presented the story through Henry's eyes we could very easily see him as a disgusting character and nothing more, but instead, while we are revolted by many of the things he says and does, we come to understand him and even to a certain extent to sympathise with him.)

There are many other ways in which the dialogue of the discussion at the party could be presented. We could, for example, hear just a snatch of it as, together with our character, we walk past. Maybe we don't need to hear much of the debate at this point, but we need to receive the impression that this debate is current, that it is in the air.

But perhaps a more interesting presentation would be to adopt the approach corresponding to that used at the start of the *The Player*, in which we – the audience – do not follow any one individual or group of characters: we are there, as it were, unaccompanied, simply roaming around. We might hear part or all of this argument or none of it; it might be presented as part of the wallpaper, part of the ambience, or it might be dwelt on at greater length, but we would be listening to it in a way that was perhaps more objective and less linked into the view of any particular character.

The *meaning* of the dialogue, then – how we interpret it – is inextricably linked with how we come across it, the viewpoint we are invited to take.

The party on stage

This last section has been written mostly from the point of view of film or television, in which the camera or microphone can make choices about what we are seeing and hearing – what is in focus. To a large extent the same can be done on radio, though of course who we are 'with' (if anyone) needs to be identified through the dialogue, where in film this can be done visually. On stage it is rather different, as we have the choice of what to look at. If, for example, we were to fill the stage with a party and tell everyone to get on with it, the audience would probably hear nothing at all with any clarity. Thus there has to be some focusing, just as the camera or microphone does this job in other media. But the fact that this has to be done differently on stage does not mean that we cannot achieve a comparable effect of slipping from one conversation to another. We do not have to limit our choice of what we hear or do not hear – we do not have to write the dialogue as a solid block – simply because this is a script for the stage.

There are two or three basic solutions to the presentation of party-type dialogue on stage. In film we can *move* from one conversation to another; on stage we can, in fact, do the same. A character can move around the performing area from one conversation to another so that these are the conversations that we hear, but as there are no microphones to do the selecting for us, the conversations which are out of focus have to fade to a much lower level of audibility (a more stylised approach might make use of freezes). Or, just as in film, instead of following a character from one conversation to another, certain pieces of dialogue may become, as it were, audible and inaudible of their own accord: our attention is drawn from one conversation to another simply on the basis of what we can hear most clearly.

Another, rather more conventional, solution – still very often used – is exemplified in the following, the stage directions at the opening of Act Two of Chekhov's *Ivanov*:

A reception room in the Lyebedevs' house; doors left, right and centre, the last leading into the garden. Expensive antique furniture. Chandeliers, candlesticks and pictures, all under dust covers.
ZEENAEDA SAVESHNA, KOSYH, AVDOTYA NAZAROVNA and YEGORUSHKA, GAVRILA, BABAKINA. Girls and elderly ladies, visitors in the house. A maid.
ZEENAEDA SAVESHNA is on a sofa; on either side of her sit elderly ladies in armchairs; the young people sit on chairs. In the background, by the door leading into the garden, several guests are playing cards; among them are KOSYH, AVDOTYA NAZAROVNA and YEGORUSHKA. GAVRILA stands by the door on the right; the maid hands round a tray of sweets and pastries. Throughout the act, the guests pass in and out from the garden and through the door on the right. BABAKINA enters through the door on the right and walks up to ZEENAEDA SAVESHNA.

Here the action stays in one place – we do not 'move', as we might in film – but the dialogue comes to us. We are with a major character (Zeenaeda Saveshna) within a group, and she is involved in dialogue not only with her immediate group but also with others as they pass through. Again, the fact that this is a party presented on stage does not mean that the variety of dialogue we can write – the number of conversations of which we may hear a part – has to be limited.

There is actually a third option in presenting party-style dialogue, particularly suited to improvised or semi-improvised theatre, though there is often an element of scripting as well. This option is to not highlight any particular piece of dialogue at all, but for there to be an element of chance as to which pieces of dialogue any particular member of the audience hears. This can work well when the play is staged in the round, and even better in a 'promenade' performance, in which the audience actually moves around within the performance area, stopping and listening to dialogue for as long as they like before moving on. When a scene is presented in this way, equal attention has to be given to the scripting (or improvisation, or mixture of the two) of every piece of dialogue taking place simultaneously.

Pace

Sometimes musical analogies may be useful. In a short piece of music, or a song, it is often perfectly satisfactory for the pace to be the same throughout. There is little or no variation necessary. If we enjoy, say, The Beatles' *She Loves You*, or Schubert's *Mein!* we do not complain that there is no change of pace: we do not have time to get bored. In a piece even a little longer, though, whether Queen's *Bohemian Rhapsody* or a Mahler symphony, we need some variation of pace. This not only avoids monotony but also allows the pace of one section to bring into stronger relief the pace of another. And some sections *need* to be slow, while others can only really work if taken at speed.

The same considerations apply in scriptwriting, although they tend to be less obvious – we don't write *Adagio* or *Presto* for different parts of a script. We need variation of pace, both in small scale and in large scale. In the small scale there needs to be variation within conversations. The most furious row may usefully be broken up by a slower, subdued, almost controlled interlude, where we know the full force of the storm must break out again. In the larger scale there needs to be contrast between whole sections. In John Osborne's *Look Back in Anger*, for example, the cutting, thrusting dialogue is offset by those parts of the play where we only hear Jimmy playing his trumpet in another room, while those present are talking things over quietly. Even in a play as full of quick and quick-witted dialogue as *Much Ado About Nothing* there are sections where the audience is allowed time to relax a little.

Let me quote further from my radio play, *A Few Kind Words*. This forty-five-minute script is divided into three scenes, each one shorter than the last. The first scene begins slowly, but then works up to a climax when Jenny refuses her father's request that she write an epitaph for her mother's gravestone. Tommy's son-in-law Roy is also present:

TOMMY: Where've yo put mah things?
JENNY: Don't be silly, Dad, you've only just got here. What I'm –
TOMMY: Wor've Ah axed from yo? Ever. Wor've Ah axed? Me uz
    brung yer up, wor've Ah axed from yo since yo've bin a
    grown woman? Nothin'. That's wor Ah've axed. And wor

am Ah axing now? Just this one... Ah'll get mi own things.

ROY: Dad all –

TOMMY: Don't yo Dad me. You've note te do wi' me.

JENNY: It's just that I can't see –

TOMMY: An' yo niver 'ave bin. Dad this Dad that, yo're summat mi dotter fahnd, an' 'er, she's not mi dotter any more, thinks of 'ersen an' nobody else. Ah don't know why Ah bothered te come dahn 'ere, thot just this time she might do summat for't family but no yo've risen above that haven't yo girl eh yo're much too high an' mighty te tek any notice of what your father might say, after all he's only –

JENNY: (*spoken simultaneous with Tommy's speech, joining in halfway through it*) Take no notice Roy, he's getting too old to argue straight any more. He'll stop in a minute and say he's sorry and expect us to forget it completely because he wants us to. He can turn it on and he can turn it off and he expects us to fit in with whenever he decides to change his –

ROY: For God's sake shut up, shut up both of you!

Dad, Mr Hetherage, whatever you want me to call you –

TOMMY: Ah'm gooin'.

JENNY: All right Dad come on let's do it, come on, let's do it.

TOMMY: (*going out of the room*) Ah'm not stoppin' 'ere te –

ROY: Look if you want your things Dad I'll get them –

JENNY: (*shouting for the first time*) I said let's do it!

(*pause*)

Come on Dad, let's sort out what we put on Mum's grave-stone. The epitaph. Do you want something light and funny...

Here, then, there is dialogue of some pace, whole speeches over-lapping with each other. Indeed, it is impossible to hear either Tommy or Jenny clearly in the two speeches which are given simul-taneously, and the impression, at least, is of considerable verbal activity.

The second scene is much slower. There are many more pauses written in between speeches, and the whole feel of the dialogue is more contemplative. The third and final scene, of which the following is an extract, is slow but intense. It is set in a nursing home:

JENNY: So what do you want?
TOMMY: From yo, nothin'.
> (*internal*) Ah wanted 'er te look at me, te look at this place...
> Ah wanted 'er te say, it's all raight Dad, Ah'm wi' yo an'
> Mum, Ah'm wi' yo. That's all Ah ever wanted. Nor 'er
> thought aht wods...
JENNY: (*internal*) To look at me and say, you're mine. A disap-
> pointment, not what I'd have wanted –
TOMMY: (*aloud*) Nothing you can give me.
JENNY: (*internal*) – but you're mine, that's all I'd want from you.
> (*aloud*) God, you're impossible to please.
TOMMY: Ow'd yo know, yo've niver tried.

Here we have a scene of tremendous conflict between two people incapable of being for each other what they would like to be, but the *pace* – in terms of speed of line delivery – is not fast. It doesn't need to be. But a whole script at this pace could be tedious. Instead, there is contrast between this and the preceding scenes and there is also contrast, both of pace and tone, within this scene, from line to line.

When it comes to performance, actors and directors will talk about pace and, quite rightly, they will not be talking merely about the speed at which the lines themselves are delivered. They will also be talking about the speed at which cues are picked up – in other words the space between one line and another. In the extract above, none of the lines would be spoken fast, but many of them would continue without any gap at all from the preceding line. This is partly a matter of interpretation but it is also a matter of you, the scriptwriter, hearing these lines in your head; and if you have heard them well, then they will probably be heard similarly by talented performers – the *meanings* will affect the pacing of cues which the performers give to them. But you can help further, simply by writing-in pauses if you wish this pace – the pace of the cues – to be slowed down, or on the other hand writing-in *overlapping*, *cutting in* or *simultaneous* where appropriate (or you can use the system demonstrated in the extract from *Top Girls* in Chapter 1). Remember that silence – pauses – allows the audience an opportunity to assimilate what has gone before, and thus can be very important. It is well known that Pinter has always been fastidious about his pauses, but so have many other writers, for the gaps between lines – in which characters themselves give time or fail to give time to consider what has gone before – can have a very powerful influence on the effectiveness of any given piece of dialogue.

Conflict, and the off switch

Let us now turn to a basic ingredient of good dialogue which we have not examined directly, although we have assumed its presence.

It hardly needs stating that dialogue needs to hold the attention of the audience. On radio and television it is very easy to switch channels, and on a number of occasions I have left cinemas and even theatres (though only at an interval) before the end of the performance. Audiences are not, in fact, captive. Yet many inexperienced scriptwriters, because they find a certain topic fascinating, or because they have a burning desire to bring a particular issue to the attention of the public, allow themselves to forget that the material must work in terms of good dialogue. *Good intentions are not enough*. We must also hold the attention of our audience.

A major ingredient in holding this attention is *conflict*. I am told that there are some societies in which art may be created out of the contemplation of peace and tranquillity. Western art, however, is not like this – even though we might wish it to be. In music, for example, there is not just contrast but an element of conflict between keys, and even the most simple musical phrase will often be based upon conflict (in the form of some discord, whether violent or mild) followed by resolution. Drama, similarly, has to have conflict, and that conflict has to make itself felt in the dialogue.

Conflict and choice

Why, though, is conflict so important? This is not easy to answer, but it is worth looking into, as otherwise we may allow ourselves to forget how central it is to drama, and we might then let ourselves produce dialogue lacking in this vital element.

Conflict implies choice. When there is conflict, we, the audience, are invited to take sides; we are invited to make a choice. Let us begin with the most straightforward conflict, the battle: in the film

Braveheart (writer, Randall Wallace) we want Wallace (Mel Gibson) to defeat the English on the battlefield. Here the conflict is clear, and whom we are meant to support is equally obvious. But we have, nevertheless, made a choice about whom we are backing. Often, though, conflicts are less clear-cut than this. We are not sure about where to place our support, or perhaps we change our minds as the performance progresses. This applies particularly to the conflicts which are quite unlike pitched battles: conflicts not between characters, but *within* them.

Staying with *Braveheart* for a moment, if we turn from Wallace to Robert the Bruce we find that, yes, he is in conflict with others, but more importantly he has conflict within himself. Bruce wants to be a man of greater integrity and less cynicism than his father, yet his father has considerable power and influence over him. Bruce wants to support Wallace unambiguously, yet is swayed by his father into taking another course, a decision which he bitterly regrets later. Bruce, then, has internal conflicts, and *these conflicts draw us in because they invite us to make choices on behalf of the characters.* Do this! No, don't do that! Don't be aggressive to her, she's your friend! You must leave that man now, whatever the consequences! Conflicts mean decisions have to be taken – by ourselves as well as by the characters. Then, we want to stay on to the end not only to see how things turn out for the character(s) with whom we empathise, but also to see if we were right in our choices.

Moment-to-moment conflict

The conflicts referred to so far are clearly part of the plot, as well as being central to the development of characterisation. But they must also be present in the dialogue. They may not necessarily be directly stated – though sometimes they are precisely that – but they must be present, in whatever form. The conflicts might be hinted at or might be displaced on to something else altogether, but nevertheless they must be there.

These are the big conflicts, the major ones which shape a whole script, but there must also be minor conflicts right the way through the dialogue (conflicts of status, of power, of control of the agenda). *These minor conflicts in the dialogue pull us in* just as do the major ones, calling on us to unravel what is going on and then inviting us to make choices on behalf of the characters.

If we present dialogue without choices, we give the audience too little to do. Furthermore, if there are no choices in the dialogue – within characters or between them (because there are no conflicts) – this also cuts down the desire of the audience to know what happens next. If instead the scriptwriter allows the dialogue to flag, if at any point he or she allows the dialogue to carry the message that all conflicts have been resolved, then the audience may well lose interest, deciding either to change channel or leave the building.

Conflict and identification

The scriptwriter must always be aware of which characters an audience is most likely to like, to empathise with, and this is not just a matter of what each character does (though of course that is extremely important). It is also a matter of what the character says, and of how it is said. More than one script has been turned down by a script editor with the comment, 'Yeah, it's great – but I just don't *like* any of the characters.' There may be the strongest plot and a thousand conflicts at every level, but if we don't like any of the characters we don't care about them, and the likelihood is that if we don't care about the characters we won't care about the production at all. Once again we will reach for the 'off' button.

We have already seen that our merely being 'with' a character produces a tendency to identify with – to side with – that character even if they might not otherwise seem particularly sympathetic. But that consideration aside, we will tend to side with characters who are attractive, and *a major element of attractiveness lies in a character's speeches.* Sometimes a character may show innate goodness through his or her dialogue, and we normally like to take the side of good people (so long as they are not insufferably good, in which case we can't identify with them at all); or they may be attractive because they are very funny, or their dialogue may be endearingly unpredictable. But we need to have attractive dialogue. However true to life a piece of scripted language may be, or however well intentioned the content, if there is not some element of attractiveness about the script then the bottom line is that the writer is unlikely to be able to sell it.

111

Conflict and the rounded character

Conflict in the dialogue ought to pull us further into the production, at the same time as increasing our identification with one or more of the characters. The character who is attacked by another but manages to come off best through witty speech is immediately more attractive, and our interest is increased. We should be wary, though, of giving all the best lines to one character, as this can lead to fighting only paper tigers – which is far from satisfying for the audience. The scriptwriter is wise to give a number of the cleverest, most attractive lines to characters with whom the audience probably does *not* identify, since then at least the hero or heroine appears to have a worthy adversary in dialogue.

An excellent example of this occurs in the film *Robin Hood, Prince of Thieves* (writers, Pen Densham and John Watson). The hero, of course, is Robin Hood (Kevin Costner), who is not only brave and good but charming as well. But the scriptwriter gives many of the most memorable lines to the Sheriff of Nottingham (Alan Rickman). All the dialogue involving this character fairly crackles, the character (and, one suspects, the actor) self-consciously delighting in the depth of his own depravity. Indeed, through the quality of his dialogue the Sheriff comes close to stealing the show. But this is no bad thing: conflict only works if it is genuine, and through the lines given to the Sheriff a fitting adversary – a *foil* – for Robin Hood is created.

Climax

Let us now look at where conflict reaches a climax within a script, and how the dialogue functions at such points. We turn once more to Arthur Miller, one of the twentieth century's greatest writers, for an example. In the First Act of *Death of A Salesman*, Miller presents us with the Loman family: Willy, Linda, Biff and Happy (along with a few other characters that we shall ignore for now). Miller could simply drop us straight into a scene involving the whole family, but he chooses not to. Instead, he first carefully shows them to us in pairs and in trios. The dialogue explores these relationships one after another: Linda and Willy; Biff and Happy; Willy with Biff and Happy in the past (though as if in the present in Willy's head); Linda and Willy again; Willy and Happy; Biff,

Happy and Linda. Only then, at the end of the Act, does he allow the four of them to talk together, and the result is an explosion.

The important element to consider here is *form*. The form that Miller has chosen has led him to present us with sections of dialogue which gradually build up to a climax. He really is like a bomb-maker, using dialogue carefully to add one ingredient after another until all are present. Then there is only the touch-paper to be lit.

However, the climax here should not be confused with the element of *pace* in dialogue. A climax takes place when a certain level of *intensity* is reached, and in order for this to be as effective as possible Miller holds back in the timing of mixing his ingredients. If a level of intensity in the dialogue is reached too early, then the remainder of the Act (or film, etc.) may feel like an anti-climax. So, however tempting it might be to let a piece of dialogue ignite whenever possible, it can be wiser to delay the high point.

The confusion of climax with pace is a common one. Again, we can turn to a musical analogy. In an eight-bar melody the high point (literally the highest note) is usually around bar seven. The same corresponding positioning of climax is often successful in scripts. But that high point in a melody may not be the moment where the music is at its *fastest*; in fact, sometimes to linger on that highest note is most effective. In Sibelius's *Seventh Symphony* the climax to the whole piece is just one, repeated, searing high note, but it is not fast and it is not loud – it is, though, tremendously *intense*. A scriptwriter makes a mistake if he or she assumes that dialogue must be at its most fast and furious to achieve the strongest climax: it is the *meaning* (and very often the conflict, of which more in a later chapter) which must be at its most intense.

Let us look at the climax to Ibsen's play, *A Doll's House*. The climax is in two parts. First there comes Helmer's discovery of the secrets that his wife Nora has been keeping from him. Here the language reflects the strength of his emotions:

HELMER: (*walking about the room*) What a horrible awakening! All these eight years – she who was my joy and pride – a hypocrite, a liar – worse, worse – a criminal! The unutterable ugliness of it all! For shame! For shame! (*NORA is silent and looks steadily at him. He stops in front of her.*) I ought to have suspected that something of the sort would happen. I

ought to have foreseen it. All your father's want of principle
– be silent! – all your father's want of principle has come out
in you. No religion, no morality, no sense of duty – How am
I punished for having winked at what he did! I did it for your
sake, and this is how you repay me.

Here, then, we have a climax of fury. The lines are probably delivered at considerable speed, and perhaps at considerable volume,
too. But the stronger climax is still to come, when just a few
minutes later Nora speaks quietly of the complete lack of communication which has always existed between them, and of her own
willingness up to this point to be first what her father had wanted
her to be, and then what her husband had wanted her to be – and
now she is going to be herself. This is a climax in which the
dialogue would sound most natural if not delivered fast, and
probably it needs no great volume, but the intensity of meaning is
very clear indeed.

8. Highly Stylised Dialogue

The hand of the author

Up to this point we have concentrated upon dialogue which has been essentially naturalistic – attempting to represent what will feel like 'realistic' dialogue, even if that is heightened from time to time. But in Chapter 6 on heightened naturalism we noted that many writers have clearly embraced forms which are non-naturalistic; forms which openly declare that they are using dialogue which is at a very clear remove from 'real life'. This is the dialogue we will be looking at in this chapter, first with a review of the two main modern non-naturalistic styles, and then moving on to some other options open to the writer of script dialogue.

Again, it must be emphasised that the dividing line between heightened naturalism and what I am calling 'highly stylised dialogue' is not entirely clear. Did anyone really ever speak like the characters in *The Big Sleep*[1], with such cool intelligence wrapped up in such lingo? Did any cowboy ever speak so few lines yet so to the point (his spits almost outnumber his lines!) as Clint Eastwood's eponymous hero in *The Outlaw Josie Wales*[2]? The answer to both questions is almost certainly 'No', but it has to be followed with 'But who cares?'. The point is that this is how we *enjoy* these characters speaking. We like the idea that in these particular worlds – here, the worlds of private detectives or of the Wild West – this is how such people spoke. Whether or not this actually *is* how people speak is of little or no importance – accuracy doesn't matter (though consistency does).

But I would still class these examples of dialogue as basically naturalistic, though using heightened naturalism. For me, *the line*

[1] Writers, William Faulkner, Leigh Brackett and Jules Furthman, from the novel by Raymond Chandler.
[2] Writers, Phil Kaufman and Sonia Chernus, from the novel by Forrest Carter.

into non-naturalism is crossed when the dialogue appears to acknowledge the hand of the author.

From a purely mercenary standpoint, it should be pointed out immediately that non-naturalism (with some notable exceptions, which we will come on to later) is much harder to sell. Some of the greatest names in scriptwriting (mainly, it has to be said, for the theatre rather than for other media) are those of writers whose work is non-naturalistic, but the public nevertheless seems generally more attuned to heightened naturalism. In order to be able to sell a non-naturalistic script the quality has to be quite exceptional. Even on the stage, the non-naturalism of the sixties and seventies is no longer generally in vogue. A much-lauded new young theatre talent like April de Angelis writes dialogue which is much closer to naturalism than that of, say, David Mowat, a similarly praised new young writer of the sixties. We have to some extent moved away from experimentalism, at least in the commercial theatre.

But there is, nevertheless, a significant amount of successful non-naturalistic scriptwriting taking place, from the films of Peter Greenaway to the stage plays of Howard Barker, and any aspiring scriptwriter should have some grasp of the variety of ways in which dialogue in this form can function.

This is not the place to embark on a history of non-naturalistic dialogue, but it might be useful at least to recognise what the trends have been. To generalise enormously, much of present non-naturalistic dialogue has sprung from two traditions – the major figure on the one hand being Brecht, and on the other being Beckett; the one tradition (initially, at least) heavily political, the other 'absurdist'. Of course, these two figures were not alone and they had their antecedents too, but for the sake of simplicity we need not be concerned with them here.

Brechtian dialogue

The term 'Brechtian' has come to mean any form of theatre employing techniques of 'alienation'. The term is also used, but to a much lesser extent, in other media. Brecht was aware that the audience was generally very ready to identify with characters, to suffer and rejoice with them and ultimately to undergo 'catharsis', a sort of purging of emotions. But at the end of all this did they actually learn anything? Were they any different at the end of the play? Had the performance genuinely changed them? Brecht was very concerned to teach his audience, so he employed techniques of 'alienation': he kept reminding them – through the visibility of all the stage equipment, through the acting style and above all through the non-naturalism of the script – that this was a *play*, that it was not real life and that therefore the response should not be as to real life. Where much theatre up to that point (and later) had simply taken away a front wall, allowing us to see a version of 'real' life in a 'real' setting, and had invited us to suspend our disbelief, Brecht did no such thing. The audience was not there to indulge itself, but to learn. Brecht was calling for an essentially intellectual rather than emotional response to his work.

This is in fact something of a caricature of Brecht's beliefs (which anyway changed over time); he recognised that some identification with characters was not always negative and that there is a place for emotional response as well, and certainly much of his dialogue is highly entertaining. But it was his constant belief that *mere* entertainment, or emotional involvement, was not enough.

The works of Brecht himself have waned in popularity somewhat, but elements of his techniques have become so much a part of the fabric of our artistic world that we take them for granted. I occasionally have individuals say to me of a documentary drama of mine, 'It's really Brechtian, isn't it?' when this had not occurred to me in such a stark form. I, along with thousands of other writers, have simply absorbed his work – it is in the atmosphere now, unavoidable. We take it for granted.

So, in terms of dialogue, what was he doing? He was aiming at clarity: characterisation is clear and so are the dilemmas into which characters are placed, so the dialogue, too, is clear. There is no sustained attempt to imitate the sloppiness of natural speech, and ambiguities of meaning – so prevalent in our everyday conversation – are mostly avoided since they would cloud the clarity of the lesson. Brecht is perfectly happy to have characters speak in quite a stilted way, and at other times in poetry or song, and for them to tell each other information which is clearly in the dialogue primarily for the benefit of the audience. He has characters speak directly to the audience and often employs what is in effect a 'chorus', or narrator(s), also speaking directly to the audience, frequently interpreting events, suggesting the conclusions we might wish to reach. If Brecht's plays often seem to have the quality of parables, the dialogue within

them, too, shares something of the quality of dialogue in fairy-tales
– poetic, symbolic and designed to present a lesson.

For a modern example of scriptwriting clearly influenced by
Brecht, we might turn to Edward Bond. The following is the
opening of his stage play, *Restoration*. We soon realise that Lord
Are is trying to strike the sort of pose taken up in a pastoral
drawing, in an attempt to impress a wealthy heiress.

> *London. The Park of LORD ARE's house.*
> *ARE and FRANK. FRANK is in livery.*

ARE: Lean me against that great thing.

FRANK: The oak sir?

ARE: Hold your tongue. No no! D'ye want me to appear drunk?
Nonchalant. As if I often spent the day leaning against an oak
or supine in the grass.

FRANK: Your lordship comfortable?

ARE: No scab I am not, if that gives ye joy. Hang my scarf over the
twig. Delicately! – as if some discriminating wind had cast it
there. Stand off. How do I look?

FRANK: Well sir... how would yer like to look?

ARE: I wore my russet and green of a purpose. Must I sprout
berries before I am at home in the landscape?

FRANK: Not seen your lordship –

ARE: Pox! Ye city vermin can't tell the difference between a
haystack and a chimney stack. Wha-ha! I must not laugh, it'll
spoil my pose. Damn! The sketch shows a flower. 'Tis too
late for the shops, I must have one from the ground.

FRANK: –What kind sir?

ARE: Rip up that pesky little thing on the path. That'll teach it to
grow where gentlemen walk.

It comes as no surprise that this script also includes many asides,
poetic speech direct to the audience and also songs, for here we are
well beyond heightened naturalism. Lord Are, attempting in his
ridiculous and unbelievable way to look the part of the country
gentleman, is speaking as no-one has ever spoken, and indeed we
are not intended to believe that anyone ever has spoken in this way.
Rather, the dialogue is about the *idea* of the character and of the
relationship between this member of the aristocracy and his servant
– it is not pretending to *be* the character and the relationship.

This, then, is the kernel of this form of dialogue. Just as in this type of theatre it is the *idea* of a carriage, a train, a pig or whatever, rather than the thing itself, that would be represented by imaginative use of props or effects on stage, so the same principle is applied to language. It is the idea of the character and the conflicts (here, class conflicts) which is communicated through the dialogue; dialogue is used for this rather than to imitate language as it ever might have been spoken. And by re-forming the language around the ideas – and in the process reminding the audience that this is language which is *made* by a writer, not merely some sort of reproduction of life – the scriptwriter is free to invite the audience to consider those ideas, those issues, rather than merely react to emotional situations. This does not mean, however, that the dialogue is just dull and teacherly. As the example shows, this style of dialogue can be as clever, witty and engaging as any other, but within a different convention. (Bizarrely, this particular extract, taken out of context, could almost be from Oscar Wilde!)

In this extract, as is often the case in the scripts of Brecht himself, the setting is an historical one. Sometimes, too, the action in these types of plays takes place in a some sort of semi-mythical place far from our own culture, as in Brecht's *The Good Woman of Setzuan* or Bond's *Narrow Road to the Deep North*. This distancing from the present day and location seems to free the scriptwriter further from any temptation merely to imitate the speech and actions of life here and now; the time and place invite the dialogue to be further removed from naturalism. It is not a coincidence that in a play like *Saved*, set in the here-and-now of the time of its writing, Bond's dialogue is utterly different – really a form of heightened naturalism rather than non-naturalism, imitating with extraordinary (and terrifying) accuracy the speech of a group of corrupt and amoral young people. Non-naturalistic dialogue certainly may be set in the here and now, but its most natural home appears to be elsewhere.

An absurd approach

The other major non-naturalistic approach to dialogue in this century has come through what is now known as 'absurd' or 'absurdist' writing. Samuel Beckett is generally accepted as being the father of this style, while many other major writers in Britain and abroad (particularly France; Beckett wrote in both English and French) have adopted a similar approach – Pinter, Ionesco, N.F. Simpson and Edward Albee among others. Rather as with Brechtian theatre, while new scripts written in a straightforwardly absurdist style are a relative rarity these days, the essence of the style appears to have soaked into the collective subconscious of the scriptwriting fraternity, so that a writer such as Stoppard can use many of the techniques of Beckett without ever being labelled an 'absurdist'. (After reading the following, the reader might like to turn again to the extract from *Albert's Bridge* on pp. 29–30, noting there some traces of the style of absurd theatre.)

The following example is from Beckett's most famous play, *Waiting for Godot*. Precisely who – or what – Godot is never becomes clear; neither is it clear why these characters are waiting for him. The set consists simply of a country road with a tree.

VLADIMIR: Well? What do we do?

ESTRAGON: Don't let's do anything. It's safer.

VLADIMIR: Let's wait and see what he says.

ESTRAGON: Who?

VLADIMIR: Godot.

ESTRAGON: Good idea.

VLADIMIR: Let's wait till we know exactly how we stand.

ESTRAGON: On the other hand it might be better to strike the iron before it freezes.

VLADIMIR: I'm curious to hear what he has to offer. Then we'll take it or leave it.

ESTRAGON: What exactly did we ask him for?

VLADIMIR: Were you not there?

ESTRAGON: I can't have been listening.

VLADIMIR: Oh... nothing very definite.

ESTRAGON: A kind of prayer.

VLADIMIR: Precisely.

ESTRAGON: A vague supplication.

VLADIMIR: Exactly.

ESTRAGON: And what did he reply?

VLADIMIR: That he'd see.

ESTRAGON: That he couldn't promise anything.

VLADIMIR: That he'd have to think it over.

ESTRAGON: In the quiet of his home.

VLADIMIR: Consult his family.
ESTRAGON: His friends.
VLADIMIR: His agents.
ESTRAGON: His correspondents.
VLADIMIR: His books.
ESTRAGON: His bank account.
VLADIMIR: Before taking a decision.
ESTRAGON: It's the normal thing.
VLADIMIR: Is it not?
ESTRAGON: I think it is.
VLADIMIR: I think so too.

Here, clearly, the situation is absurd – the two characters waiting for another character for no clear reason. But the absurdity of the situation should not blind us to the absurd nature of the dialogue, too. This is conversation between people who are pretending to understand their position, yet who don't. In this extract Estragon appears at the start to know what Vladimir is talking about, but then in the fourth line it becomes clear that he does not. Then the two of them go on to try to convince each other that they know what they have asked Godot for and what his response was – though it's not really clear that they have ever even met him. Yet even all this, very strange though it is, could have been couched in a form of dialogue close to everyday, natural speech, but it is not. The cliché, 'Strike while the iron is hot' is mangled by Estragon (in naturalistic dialogue it would surely be presented in its normal form, but in this world no-one has a full command of language or meaning); then at times it is as if one sentence has been chopped up and been split between the two of them – the undisguised artificiality is clear. Yet the beauty of this type of writing, when it is well done, is not that it is merely weird but that the dialogue does, nevertheless, faithfully communicate the essence of how characters who are lost, who don't know where to turn, really do talk to each other. Again – though in a very different form from that of Brechtian theatre – we are dealing with essences.

So what are the implications for us, as scriptwriters, if we choose to make use of this type of dialogue? First we should bear in mind that whenever it is used it has the strong tendency to carry the meaning – whatever the words do or do not actually *say* – that these characters are trying but failing to make sense of the world.

Indeed, in *Waiting for Godot* we gain the very strong impression that this is because it is actually impossible to make sense of the world; all we can do is come up with more or less convincing rationalisations for what goes on, attempting to convince ourselves that we understand our existences.

Similarly, in Stoppard's *Rosencrantz and Guildenstern are Dead*, we have two characters who find themselves as virtual walk-ons, while the real action in life is taking place elsewhere; both are trying and failing to make sense of this and trying to avoid their inevitable fate (they can't, and we know what it is if we have seen *Hamlet*). Or in Ionesco's *Rhinoceros* a whole society is busy rationalising the gradual change of the population into rhinoceroses; to us this may appear to be about society being taken over by vulgarians (or possibly even fascists), but the meaning is never spelled out. *Thus, in absurd dialogue there is always a great deal of ambiguity; meanings are never clear.*

But all these scripts do seem to have in common the belief that communication through language between individuals, and real understanding between them, is extremely difficult. It is as if in absurd dialogue the language resonates, and the characters can only do their best to pick up the resonances – direct communication appears not to work.

So this, then, is the territory we are entering if as scriptwriters we choose to employ this style of dialogue. It is an option open to us, but – whatever else our script may be saying – it is difficult to avoid these meanings which seem to be in common in scripts written in this style.

Yet, despite this, 'theatre of the absurd' is very far from being all the same. Harold Pinter, for example, particularly in his early work, manages to forge a remarkable combination of absurd-type dialogue with speech that at the same time appears to be a high point of closely observed naturalistic speech. Most of his early scripts present characters from close to the bottom of the social scale, and he is able to produce a type of dialogue which both imitates the incoherence of many of these individuals and at the same time seems to be quite 'absurd'; motivations and meanings – and very often tremendous aggression – are here expressed not so much *through* the words as *under* them. *And here, as elsewhere, 'absurd' dialogue is predominantly the speech of those who feel they have very little control over their lives.* On some occasions another layer of stylised non-naturalism is added through the repetition of phrases and even whole speeches (again almost as if they were passages of music, as noted in Chapter 5). 'Absurd' dialogue may, then, be combined with something like a certain naturalism, but again it is consistency of style that is important. A simple mixing of 'absurd' dialogue with sections which might sound like, say, David Hare, would produce something quite indigestible.

From the comic books

The Brechtian and 'absurd' traditions offer two of the main options for scriptwriters of non-naturalistic dialogue, but there are also others. One that has become particularly popular in recent years has evolved from comic books, leading to films and television series such as *Batman, Superman, Dick Tracy* and *Spiderman*. In these productions many of the events – and, of course, many of the characters, as well as the settings – are brazenly non-naturalistic. With Superman zooming up to explode an asteroid that is threatening Earth, Batman inhabiting the ultra-gothic Gotham City and even the colours used in the film of *Dick Tracy* screaming high stylisation, one might expect a corresponding approach in the dialogue. Rather surprisingly, though, the dialogue in these scripts tends to be their most naturalistic element. The characters may be mentioning phenomena which to us seem impossible or at least utterly futuristic, yet the language in which they express themselves is hardly stylised. In some versions (the older *Batman* television series comes to mind) there is an imitation of the comics' 'Aaaaaaaaagh!' or 'WHACK!!!', splashed across the screen as words, but generally scriptwriters seem to have realised – particularly when dealing with feature-length films – that while these may work well on the page in relatively short comic strips, they can easily become tedious when repeated in another medium. Sometimes there is a certain division between naturalistic speech for the main 'positive' characters and much more stylised speech for the villains. Here the type of dialogue employed emphasises the 'otherness' of the villains – thus making them even less appealing and more luridly villainous – while the more naturalistic speech of the heroes or heroines seems to make them more like ourselves, and thus strengthens our empathy with them. In the television series

The New Adventures of Superman the dialogue between Lois and Clark and the rest of the staff at the 'Daily Planet' may be clever, witty and at times even laced with irony, but it is essentially a heightened naturalism with which we can identify; it is the ever-changing gallery of villains who employ extreme styles of speech, distancing us from them even further.

In the related genre of science fiction some attempts have been made to script dialogue in a form as stylised as the rest of the production. These range from the guttural sounds of the Klingons in the *Star Trek* series of films to the impressively sophisticated Future-Anglo-Russian-speak in Stanley Kubrick's film *A Clockwork Orange* (the language, of course, comes originally from the novel by Anthony Burgess). The option for highly stylised dialogue in these forms certainly exists, though few scriptwriters take advantage of it.

Poetic dialogue

In general, if scripts using highly stylised dialogue are the hardest to sell, then scripts using poetic dialogue are the hardest to sell of the hardest to sell. We may all greatly admire *Under Milk Wood* or the work of Tony Harrison or, for that matter, *Murder in the Cathedral*, but in our own time there is really hardly any market for poetic dialogue. In fact, if one were to give a single piece of advice on how not to have your script accepted, it would be to write it in poetry.

But again, there are exceptions, particularly on the stage, and they vary enormously. Tony Harrison has already been mentioned, but there are others such as the Caribbean writer Derek Walcott, slipping back and forth from poetry to prose in, for example, *Ti-Jean and His Brothers*; or there is the muscular, obscene and dynamic poetic dialogue of Steven Berkoff in plays like *East* and *Greek*. Clearly in all these scripts, as in the Dylan Thomas play, there is a real delight in the use of language for its own sake, but for those determined to write poetic dialogue the strongest piece of advice – actually born out by these scripts – must be not to be self-indulgent. *The poetry, however stunning in itself, must always be at the service of the drama.* Just as in all other forms of dialogue, it must always be developing character, plot or some other aspect of the drama (in whatever way – obscure, subtle or otherwise).

Words for their own sake – whether poetry or prose – are not enough. And when you read these successful poetic scripts you see that every flourish of rhetoric is, in fact, at the service of some other aspect of the script; there are no *mere* words.

Romeos and Juliets

Let us complete this chapter with a glance at an excellent example of where non-naturalistic dialogue has been combined with other equally non-naturalistic elements.

In Shakespeare's time it was the norm to write dialogue in poetic form. Marlowe, Jonson, Webster and others all had their characters speak in poetry. Now, of course, it is far from the norm. But perhaps we may learn a little from how this poetic speech may be presented to a modern audience.

Baz Luhrmann has adapted *Romeo and Juliet* for the big screen, set in modern times with guns, helicopters and all. He could have rewritten the dialogue in the same way as it was rewritten for *West Side Story* (itself using clearly stylised language), or he could, instead, have reworked the dialogue into a more naturalistic modern idiom. Instead, in his film Luhrmann keeps to the precise language of the original, opting only to edit (as, after all, often happens in stage productions). The result is extraordinary – television commentators speaking utterly non-naturalistic Elizabethan poetry, drivers of beaten-up motors speaking the language of the 1590s. Yet it works marvellously, as it is done with real commitment and flair. The idea of antique dialogue in a thoroughly modern context may seem odd, but in fact the result is satisfying *because the non-naturalistic dialogue matches extremely well the equally non-naturalistic visual presentation* – the florid, exaggerated sets and costumes, the jarring cuts, the pieces of film running at double speed and a host of other consciously cinematic effects. It is with all this that the language of the dialogue is of a piece: we very soon realise that 'in-your-face' non-naturalism is the convention established by the film – and we accept it. So, if we are considering writing dialogue in non-naturalistic or even poetic form, we come back to the same lesson: what is demanded is consistency of approach, such as is delivered in this film.

9. The Character Tells the Story

Two types of narration

We noted in an earlier chapter that there is no narrator in life – we have to find our way through it as best we can without such assistance. Similarly, scripts have to be negotiated by the audience mostly without the aid of a narrator. At the same time, however, there is something comforting about narration. It can lend a certain air of security, so that the audience feels that at least someone knows what is going on. For this reason and others (which will be discussed later), many scriptwriters have used a variety of forms of narration within the dialogue.

In examining narration we should first make a clear distinction between narration from within character and so-called 'impersonal' narration. In the former, a character is speaking direct to the audience, as a sort of aside. On stage this is normally a character quite literally turning to the audience to make a comment; on television and in film, character-narration is usually presented through voice-over (as in innumerable French films), but there are a number of notable exceptions where the narration is to camera. On radio it is a matter of a change of microphone and acoustic, making it clear that this character is somehow outside the scene at this moment. 'Impersonal' narration, on the other hand, involves using a speaker who is not a character within the drama.

Impersonal narration

These two types of narration produce very different effects. Most of this chapter will examine the use of narration from within character, but here we will look just briefly at 'impersonal' narration. This is generally rarely used now, although a form of it does arise occasionally as 'chorus'. Sometimes, too, in films (as in *Casablanca*) there is a brief use of impersonal narration, particularly at the start

– comparable to the prologue in an Elizabethan stage play – and at the ending, though these often take the form of on-screen writing rather than voice-over. The problem with the impersonal voice-over is that it is not, in fact, impersonal in the same way that an impersonal narrator in a novel might appear to be. In film or in other script media we hear a real voice, so it ceases immediately to be impersonal – we want to know whose voice this is, and perhaps even why it is making the statement.

There are some successful uses of impersonal narration in modern script media. For example, in his play *The Fire Raisers* Frisch makes effective use of a chorus of unidentifiable individuals (an inheritance from Greek theatre); in fact, it is immediately clear that the narration is not truly 'impersonal', since the chorus represents the guardians of the city – and, by extension, of the civilisation. Similarly, the memorable opening to *Citizen Kane* (writers, Herman J. Mankiewicz and Orson Welles) uses what seems to be an impersonal narrator, but we soon come to identify the voice and speech style with newsreel used at other points in the film; the narration is part of a broader quasi-documentary effect. In the film *Jules et Jim* (writers, François Truffaut and Jean Gruault) there is, for once, a genuinely impersonal narrator, giving at least an impression of cool detachment, a clear view on highly emotional events. But this is a rarity in the script media; it is much more common – and generally much more successful – where there is narration at all, for that narration to come from within character.

The character-narrator

In the theatre, there are many examples of character-narration in both Elizabethan and modern drama. Both the soliloquy and the short aside are common in the work of Shakespeare and his contemporaries, while in modern drama which has been even vaguely influenced by Brecht, character-narration direct to the audience is an accepted part of the style. The more strictly naturalistic school tends not to make use of it, however, as it jars somewhat with the manner of the rest of the production. Where film and television are concerned, while a character suddenly speaking direct to camera seems somewhat outrageous and so is not often used, occasionally it does work well, as in the *Carry On* films. Often it is reserved for endings, as in the tongue-in-cheek conclusion to *Robin Hood, Prince of Thieves*, or the last line of *Devil's Advocate* (writers, Jonathan Lemkin and Tony Gilroy) in which the Devil (Al Pacino) turns to camera to remark that vanity really is his favourite sin. Perhaps the technique is so often left for the end of the film because stylistic consistency would demand that any earlier use be followed by further usage, which would be very difficult to successfully accomplish while maintaining an otherwise essentially naturalistic presentation. However, there are one or two successful examples of consistent narration to camera, such as the the television series for teenagers *As If*, or the film *High Fidelity* (writers, D.V. DeVincentis and Nick Hornby). In general, though, contemporary film and television scripts tend to make far more use of character-narration as voice-over.

So, if we are to pepper our dialogue with voice-over character-narration, what are its uses, and what are its dangers?

We noted earlier, in Chapter 7, one effect of character-narration: it tends to increase the audience's identification with the character who is narrating. To turn once more to *Goodfellas*, here we have a gangster, Henry, narrating his life to us – a life of violence, crime, selfishness, abuse of his wife and betrayal. Yet the fact that it is Henry narrating this to us, Henry telling us the story in his own words, does nevertheless create a bond between audience and character: we are to some extent on his side, despite everything. There is something similar in *The Opposite of Sex* (writer, Don Roos) where our anti-heroine, Dedee, is really very unpleasant to all those around her, but her voice-over narration is so wickedly funny that we find ourselves empathising with her anyway.

We see a great deal of both Henry in *Goodfellas* and Dedee in *The Opposite of Sex* and their narrations work extremely well. A less successful example of character-narration, though, occurs in Arthur Miller's play *A View from the Bridge*. The problem with the character-narrator here, Alfieri, lies in the ratio of narration to other speech. We simply do not see enough of Alfieri *apart* from his role as narrator for him to be firmly established as a character in his own right. The result is that he appears to be too much a device rather than a character. Miller has fallen between two stools: Alfieri is neither an impersonal narrator, outside the action, nor a convincing character-narrator.

128

The character-narrator and time

Now let us turn once more to the extract from early in the script of Woody Allen's *Annie Hall* (*see* pp. 97–8). Here we have Alvy as voice-over narrating events that took place when he was a child. The important point here is that it is Alvy as an adult narrating the events of his own childhood. Looking back on things often has a certain moving quality (it is the attraction of reminiscence); the past of any individual can never be recaptured or changed. Yet we want to capture it again, and we want to change it. We want to be able to live the wonderful moments once more, and the fact that we never can – all we can ever have is the memory – is moving. At the same time, we want to be able to change those things which went badly wrong, we want to be able to relive our lives in the light of what we have subsequently found out, but once again this is impossible, and that impossibility too is moving. So narration from a character looking back at their own experiences tends to have a very strong emotional appeal – stronger than that of a narrator concentrating on the experiences of others. So it is important here that it is the adult Alvy looking back at *himself*. Then, as we noted earlier, Allen takes this further, having impossible interaction between the characters of then and now, which is humorous but at the same time also adds to the pathos (although this is pathos with a light touch) because we know, of course, that it is precisely this sort of interaction that is impossible. (The appeal here has something in common with that of both *Groundhog Day* and *Summersby*, both of which in their very different ways present the possibility of leading life again, without the mistakes of the past.)

This question of narration and time is a complex one. The scriptwriter who decides to use character-narration in the dialogue has to decide *from when* the character is narrating. A character can narrate from the very moment of the action, speaking in the present tense, so that it becomes a sort of personal running commentary. This can certainly work well, and indeed Allen himself uses it on more than one occasion; it is particularly effective later in *Annie Hall*, presenting the thoughts – popping up on to the screen as written words – of two characters while they are out on a first date. But that is the point: whether as voice-over or as writing, this is narration as *thoughts*, at the very moment when the events are happening. Certainly there is a place for this form of narration in dialogue, but it has its limitations: it does not have that moving quality of looking back; *nor does it afford the opportunity for the narrator to have thought about these events since they have happened*, and therefore to have come to some conclusions about them.

Multiple narrators

Sometimes there is more than one narrator in a script. In Michael Frayn's *Copenhagen*, for example, the narration shifts fluidly between the three characters; it is usually the character who is least directly involved in the action at that moment who takes on the narration. The play is set after the death of all three characters; each of them is giving his or her interpretation of the momentous events of many years ago. So, while sometimes their recollections and understandings dovetail happily, at other times they do not tie in at all. The play is about interpretations, of Science and of History. The multiple narration underscores that the play is not, ultimately, about facts, but about how these facts are viewed.

My own radio play, *Corridor*, is set in a prison, during the half-hour which was at that time allowed for a visit (it is a thirty-minute play). The two characters have spent much of the visit so far arguing, and Roy has just given a fifteen-line rant on how he doesn't regret his life of petty crime and has no intention of reforming. It then continues:

MAUREEN: You're not the man I married, Roy.
ROY: That's right. Things have changed a bit since then.
MAUREEN: Prison's done something to you.
ROY: It does something to everyone.
    (*internal*) For some –
MAUREEN: Roy can't you take your mind off prison and pinching bloody televisions?
ROY: (*internal*) – it's like a school. They go there every few years for a bit of training when they're falling behind the times.
MAUREEN: There's years of your life left, our lives left. Can't you think about that?
ROY: (*internal*) Others, it makes them curl up, pathetic –
MAUREEN: (*brightly*) I was talking to Joe Chipperfield the other day.

ROY: Oh yeah?

> (*internal*) – you watch them drying up in front of you. By the time they leave –

MAUREEN: Saying he was fed up with kids working in the shop – unreliable, never stay more than a few months, and they can hardly add up.

> (*internal*) I don't know if it was then that I realised.

ROY: (*internal*) – they're no good for anything, dried up old apples.

MAUREEN: Anyway, cut a long story short –

> (*internal*) It might have been. It might have been before the visit started.
>
> (*aloud*) – he says he'd like to have you working for him when you come out.

ROY: (*internal*) Kicked about outside and end up back here again. And some finish up like me. Got to hold on.

> (*aloud*) Joe Chipperfield?

MAUREEN: Yes.

ROY: Ha!

MAUREEN: (*internal*) But I knew I wouldn't visit him again.

ROY: His Dad gave us a beating for nicking apples out of his precious orchard. I wouldn't have worked in his lousy shop if he paid me. I suppose he would have paid me. Or maybe he'd have been showing enough of his big heart by letting me work there for nothing – permission to be in his holy shop at all would have been enough.

MAUREEN: He says he doesn't mind about what you've done in the past –

[ROY: (*internal*) And what had it got to do with him?]*

MAUREEN: Says it doesn't make any difference, as far as he's concerned.

> * *This line deleted in rehearsal.*

Here we have two narrators operating at the same time, both looking back on the one occasion from very different perspectives. This technique can produce fascinating results, as we are aware not only of the 'present' – the scene as it is happening – but also of two different perspectives from the future. The contrasts between these perspectives is much starker when presented like this – as the 'present' is happening – than would be the case if the scriptwriter instead had merely moved on to a later period of their lives and allowed us to learn their views at that point. It is this jarring mix of simultaneous perspectives which is so effective.

Roy's narration is in the past tense, so it is looking back from a future point, but at times it also has some of the quality of thoughts at that moment. It is as if, looking back on that occasion, he not only gives us his views from this later 'now' looking back, but he is also reminded of what he thought at the time. So there is a certain ambiguity here, a mixing of his thoughts of now and then. In addition, parts of his narration are in fact in the present tense, even though he is looking back. As we noted in an earlier chapter, a person telling a story will often slip into the present tense, as they are reliving the moment and also making it more vivid for the listeners. So there is an element of that here. But there is more than that: Roy's use of the present tense implies a continuity – that things are *still* like this in prison, and this prepares us for the fact that although Roy is looking back on this occasion from a future time, at that future time he is also in prison – he is back inside again.

I have included here a line which I decided to cut during rehearsals. This is because it was confusing. On hearing the actor give the line I realised something that I should have realised earlier – that however well delivered by the actor (in this case the excellent Kenneth Cranham), it would be unclear to the audience whether this line was 'internal' or spoken to Maureen. A great deal can be done with a change of microphone and change of acoustic, as well as a change of tone of voice on the part of the actor, but here the line itself was too misleading – it had to go. The distinction between speech to the audience and speech to another character must be a clear one.

Narration from a point in the future looking back allows us – at the end of the script, or sometimes earlier – to catch up with this 'now', the 'now' that is the point from which the character is looking back. So in *Corridor*, for example, we find out at the end that Maureen has split up with Roy and is now living with another man, while catching up with the 'now' of Roy only leaves us in prison once again.

A new scene, a new narrator

There are some scripts in which narrators are not mixed together, as in *Corridor*, but where instead different characters narrate different sections of the script. This is a device more common in the novel than in scripts, but in scripts, too, it can be very effective.

We have already referred to *A Few Kind Words*, the first long scene of which is narrated by Tommy, the old Derbyshire miner. The second scene, though, is narrated by his daughter, Jenny. This pushes us into seeing the relationship from a new perspective. Then only in the final scene do we have the two characters narrating together. Tommy is now dying, in a home. Until this scene, Jenny has refused to produce an inscription for the headstone for her mother's grave – the 'few kind words' Tommy has wanted from her. Now, however, she has come along with a possible inscription – 'You lived the life you had to live. We loved you for it' – but Tommy hates it. Here, then, is the ending of the play:

JENNY: So what do you want?
TOMMY: From yo, nothin'.
    (*internal*) Ah wanted 'er te look at me, te look at this place... Ah wanted 'er te say, it's all raight Dad, Ah'm wi' yo an' Mum, Ah'm wi' yo. That's all Ah ever wanted. Nor 'er thought aht wods...
JENNY: (*internal*) To look at me and say, you're mine. A disappointment, not what I'd have wanted –
TOMMY: (*aloud*) Nothing yo can give me.
JENNY: (*internal*) – but you're mine, that's all I'd wanted from you.
    (*aloud*) God you're impossible to please.
TOMMY: 'Ow'd yo know, yo've niver tried.
    (*pause*)
    Lived the life she 'ad te live. What's that make me? Slave driver?
JENNY: We all live the lives we've got to.
TOMMY: An' what's the use of puttin' that on't gravestone?
JENNY: What's the <u>use</u> of anything? It just happens. I'm trying to stop blaming people.
TOMMY: What's there te blame for?
JENNY: (*internal, with control*) This was –
TOMMY: Did she live such a terrible life?
JENNY: She was a collier's wife.
    (*internal*) – the last time –
TOMMY: An' wer that such an awful thing?

JENNY: (*internal*) – and I couldn't –
(*aloud*) It wasn't her fault, it wasn't your fault –
TOMMY: Yo with yer perfect broken marriage an' yer job that
does no-one any good –
JENNY: (*internal*) – do any better –
(*aloud*) It does do some good.
TOMMY: An' yo sit theer lecturin' me –
JENNY: (*internal*) – do any better –
TOMMY: – on 'ow uz we've gorra live lahk this or live lahk that
–
JENNY: (*internal*) – do any better –
TOMMY: Well Ah'm tellin' yo that we live 'ow we want te live, an'
we die 'ow we want te die, an' fer me that's wi' yo not 'ere.
JENNY: (*internal*) – than this.
pause
TOMMY: (*internal*) A few kind words –
JENNY: (*internal*) – that's all I wanted.

This use of double narration within dialogue produces a very powerful effect of dramatic irony – we know the perspectives of each of the
characters, but neither of them truly knows that of the other. In this
particular script the clash of the two sets of narration has been held
back for the end of the play, which increases the emotional impact.
And we find out that in fact there are strong similarities between the
two: 'a few kind words' are not only what is needed for the grave-
stone, but are also what each of them desperately wants from the
other but is incapable of giving – they cannot stop themselves from
being aggressive with each other. At the very end of the play their
feelings are at heart so similar – despite their conflict – that they even
share one line between them, Tommy beginning it and Jenny finishing it. *We hear all this, but the characters don't, and it is this which
adds so greatly to the effectiveness of the scene.*

One other small point may be made here, although not specifically related to narration. Jenny repeats the phrase 'do any better'
a number of times. It has been noted earlier that repeated lines or
even whole speeches can take on new meanings each time, but here
the effect is rather different. On each repetition the line acquires
more and more power, but leading finally only to 'than this' – a
horrible anti-climax that can only be followed by a pause.
Repetition in dialogue, then, can be an extremely versatile tool.

A shared experience

We have seen in the previous example that a line may sometimes be shared by two characters. We saw a very different example (though not of narration) that also felt like lines shared between two in *Waiting for Godot*. Lines may, in fact, be split between a larger number of characters.

Let us take a speech that we have decided to give to a character in a stage play, speaking to the audience:

> *As JOYCE speaks we see a number of women taking things to the pawnbroker's, and a couple of well dressed ladies walk past.*

JOYCE: We used to go down the pawn shop, every week. Take his best trousers in on the Monday, get 'em out again the end of the week. And if things got really hard, we'd take in other bits and pieces as well – my grandfather's watch, I remember. Sometimes we'd not get things back. Couldn't afford to. And you'd see the toffs walkin' down the street, watchin' you as you went in. But I'd look up, I would. I'd look 'em in the eye.

This speech works perfectly well as a piece of narration. Perhaps at the same time we are seeing something of what she is describing. But now let's split the lines up.

> *As JOYCE speaks we see a number of women taking things to the pawnbroker's, and a couple of well dressed ladies walk past.*

JOYCE: We used to go down the pawn shop, every week.
ALICE: Take his best trousers in on the Monday –
JOYCE: – get 'em out again the end of the week.
SARAH: And if things got really hard, we'd take in other bits and pieces as well –
ANNE: – my grandfather's watch, I remember.
SARAH: Sometimes we'd not get things back. Couldn't afford to.
JOYCE: And you'd see the toffs walkin' down the street –
ALICE: – watchin' you as you went in.
JOYCE: But I'd look up, I would. I'd look 'em in the eye.

Now, with the lines clearly split between a number of characters, we have the effect of a truly shared experience: the sharing of the lines seems to symbolise the sharing of this aspect of their lives. But the lines are not split at random. The passage is still dominated by Joyce, who begins and ends it, and is given the most memorable line (in this case the final one). And the sentences about taking in other things and perhaps not getting them back are shared by Sarah and Anne – very gently implying that these characters have more experience of this than the others. A completely random distribution of lines tends to lend uniformity, which is not quite the intention.

Now we may experiment with taking it a stage further.

JOYCE and ALICE are taking trousers to the pawnbroker's.

JOYCE: We used to go down the pawn shop, every week.
ALICE: – down the pawn shop, every week. Take his best trousers in on the Monday –
JOYCE: – in on the Monday, get 'em out again the end of the week.
Reluctantly producing more items –
SARAH: And if things got really hard, we'd take in other bits –
ANNE: – and pieces
SARAH: – as well.
ANNE: My grandfather's watch, I remember.
SARAH: Sometimes we'd not get things back. Couldn't afford to.
JOYCE: And you'd see the toffs –
SARAH: – the toffs –
ANNE: – the toffs –
ALICE: – the toffs –
ALL: – the toffs! –
Two well dressed ladies appear, and watch the others.
JOYCE: – walkin' down the street –
ALICE: – watchin' you as you went in.
JOYCE: But I'd look up, I would. I'd look 'em in the eye.

Now repetition is used to further emphasise the shared nature of the experience, and there is more detailed splitting up of the lines, serving here to stress the meaning: the slight awkwardness produced by splitting the line 'bits/ – and pieces / – as well' draws

136

attention to the reluctance of these characters to keep going, to do it, to produce these items and take them to the pawn shop.

Dangers in character-narration

So, the use of character-narration certainly opens up opportunities for the scriptwriter. But there are dangers here, too.

The first danger is that, poorly used, character-narration can seem opportunistic. It can give the impression that the writer is stuck, cannot think of any way of communicating a certain piece of information through dialogue or action and so throws a piece of narration into the mouth of a character. At worst, some scripts are actually like this, though mercifully, most of them are not produced!

This tendency is most often seen in radio writing. As we have noted earlier, many inexperienced writers for radio seem to believe that it is important for us to be given all the information that we might receive visually were the script intended for any other medium, but they don't see how it can be done. They don't want to stuff the information into ordinary conversation as it would sound false. Solution? Have someone simply tell us it all – throw in a bit of narration. But in fact we must go back to our earlier point: invariably, almost all the information imparted for this reason is irrelevant; we hardly ever need to know what people or things look like, for example, since we would rather imagine them for ourselves. And most other details, if we really need to know them, we can gather from the implications of normal dialogue.

But perhaps it is the actual storyline that the radio writer is having trouble conveying:

> *Acoustic as for bedroom. We hear night sounds, perhaps an owl, and a ticking clock.*
> CAROL: Why can't I sleep? Why can I never get a decent night's sleep?
> (*pause*)
> Oh, I'll go and get myself a glass of milk, I think it's my stomach playing me up.
> *We hear CAROL getting out of bed, going down the stairs, going into the kitchen, taking milk out of the fridge and pouring it.*

CAROL: My God, there's someone in the garden. I'm sure there is – there's someone in the garden. There's someone in the garden. What do I do? He's seen me! He must have seen me! But maybe it's not... Maybe it's nobody. Maybe it's just shadows... Yeah, there's nothing there, there's nothing there.

This is very poor writing. The scriptwriter has come across a problem: when there is only one person present in a radio play – and of course you can't *see* anything – how do you tell the audience what is happening? The solution should not be to have a character talking to herself – it sounds utterly false and opportunistic. Instead, there are at least two other possible solutions. The first is the simplest: change the story, either cutting this incident altogether or radically altering it to include someone else; perhaps, for example, the scene could open with Carol on the phone, panicking, telling a friend (or maybe even the police) that she is watching – at this very second – a man in her garden in the middle of the night. The second solution, if the writer is certain that this part of the story cannot be altered, is to let us find out about the incident afterwards. Use a bit of telling rather than showing. So the following day Carol tells her colleague, friend or relation that she thought she saw this man, though it might only have been shadows.

Here we should make clear distinctions between the following: a character speaking to the audience, telling a piece of the story; the audience hearing the thoughts of a character, given as the events are happening; a character speaking to him- or herself. We have already seen the ways in which the first two may work, but the third is almost always a failure. After all, in normal life we do tell each other stories and we do have thoughts, but we very rarely speak to ourselves at any length. Yet why then, it might be asked, does a soliloquy such as 'To be or not to be...' work so well? The reason is that, although in a sense Hamlet is talking to himself, these are essentially his thoughts, a reflection of his state of mind. *Character-narration works best when it is essentially telling us about state of mind, and is at its worst when it is basically a running commentary.*

138

Establishing the convention

We have noted in many other contexts that a script establishes its own conventions of use of language, and that consistency of style is then vital. This is particularly so in the case of character-narration. If one is going to use this technique, one must establish the convention very early in the script; otherwise, the first time a character speaks direct to the audience it will appear very odd indeed. Similarly, once use of the convention has been established, it must be adhered to. It will not work if only used very occasionally.

And one last word on narration: it has to be just as engaging as all the rest of the dialogue. It is not good enough to think that the really interesting exchanges happen between people, whereas the boring background stuff can go into narration: *narration has to be as alive as all the rest*. In this respect as in every other, narration must never be thought of as an easy option.

10. Comic Dialogue

The context of comic dialogue

It is notoriously difficult to pin down exactly how comedy works. Why, exactly do we laugh? What, for us human beings, is the function of laughter – what exactly are we doing it for? Well, fortunately here we do not have to come up with the answers to these questions; just as in order to turn a set of lights on you do not need to know the physics of how electricity and light rays work, so in order to write comic dialogue you do not need to know the theories of how it might be that humour works. But you do need to know where you might find the switches. In this chapter we will find some of the switches for comic dialogue – and check that we know how to flick them.

First, we have to make a distinction between *comedy* and *comic dialogue*. Of course, it is possible to create comedy with no dialogue at all – mimes do it, and clowns, and Buster Keaton was pretty successful at it, too. And then when there is dialogue in comedy, it is not the only ingredient of the humour. Sometimes the dialogue does work virtually alone, but much more often it is only effective because of how the language reflects upon character, or has an effect upon plot, or interacts with other elements – visual, musical, whatever. In short, comic dialogue takes place within a context, and *the humour arises from the particular language in the particular context*. Even stand-up comedians, whom one might think of as simply telling jokes, like to create a 'persona', a character particularly suited to their type of humour. It is not just the lines themselves which create the laughs. For example, think of the personae of stand-up comedians Ben Elton on the one hand and Ken Dodd on the other. The comic lines of Elton would cease to be comic if presented within the persona of Dodd, and vice-versa. They wouldn't work. *The context in which the lines are presented is crucial.*

Similarly, comic dialogue is not merely a succession of jokes: in fact, *exactly the same line in two different scripts might come across as funny in one, as serious in the other*. Let us take, for example, a piece of dialogue which we looked at when discussing status, in Chapter 2. Here we had three characters, each subtly attempting to raise their own status at the expense of that of the others. Our analysis of the passage was straightforward, and assumed that this was not a particularly comic piece of dialogue. But here it is again, below, this time with the two sections printed without a break. When you read it, think of it in a different context; think of it as comedy. Remember, a comic script is always read (or heard or seen) with the expectation that it will be funny – this allows us to *hear* the lines differently. And for this passage let us assume that certain exaggerated character traits have already been established:

- John is a brainless twit, though a twit with money;
- Andy always likes to be the centre of attention, and has a tendency to patronise;
- Tim is a snob who generally considers himself superior not only to these two but to the rest of humanity in general.

At the start, then, Andy is extremely patronising to John, and enjoys drawing attention to himself as soon as possible. And later Tim is very far from happy that John, this brainless twit, is outshining him by buying a yacht, so Tim does his best to limit the damage to his ego.

Now, bearing all this in mind, try reading this as part of a comic script:

JOHN: It was terrible. I thought I was going to get stuck under the boat!
ANDY: That's really scary, isn't it, when you capsize.
JOHN: It certainly is!
TIM: At least the first time.
ANDY: I remember once when we went over I actually was stuck under the boat – only for a while of course. And it was in October.
TIM: The water must have been freezing.
ANDY: It was.
TIM: I was hit by the boom once. I was actually unconscious. It's just incredibly lucky that I wasn't sailing single-handed or –

ANDY: (*laughing*) But it's a bit stupid letting yourself get hit by the boom, isn't it?

TIM: (*laughing*) I had a hell of a bump on my head, I can tell you! (*slight pause*)

JOHN: You know that money I inherited.

ANDY: Nnn.

JOHN: Well I'm thinking of buying a yacht.

ANDY: A yacht?!

JOHN: Only a small one. About thirty foot.

ANDY: Doesn't sound that small to me. But... would you know how to sail it?

JOHN: There are training courses. I'd go on one of those. I don't suppose it's all that difficult, but you ought to learn properly, if you're going to be serious about it, don't you think?

ANDY: Well yes, I suppose you're right.

TIM: So are you completely set on this?

JOHN: Not totally.

TIM: Only – don't get me wrong – I mean I've been on yachts a number of times, and it's great, but it's not quite as exciting as dinghy sailing. It's a bit more sedate really. Well it's bound to be isn't it. You're not leaping around the whole –

JOHN: (*overlapping*) But I don't think I want to be leaping around the whole time.

TIM: Fine. Well, maybe... maybe a yacht's the thing for you then.

Perhaps to enhance the humorous effect one might want to tweak a line here or there, but this passage – read as part of a comedy, with lines now heard in the context of clear and exaggerated characterisation – is already using a major ingredient of comic dialogue: status games. The fact that many people put a great deal of energy into trying to raise their own status and lower that of others was noted when this passage was first considered, in a non-comic context; in a comic context status becomes – if anything – an even more important consideration.

Status and comedy

A huge variety of comic dialogue plays with the idea of status. Sometimes the humour arises from the reduction in status of those who genuinely do have it; but far more common is the character

142

who speaks (and acts) as if he or she had some sort of high status, when in fact they do not. Thus Captain Mannering's lines in *Dad's Army* are amusing to a large extent because we know – and he doesn't – that he is really not a very important person (the same applies in *The Brittas Empire*). The comic effect lies in the distance between his view of himself and our view of him. Sometimes Harold Steptoe in *Steptoe and Son* (writers, Ray Galton and Alan Simpson) has lines which are similarly amusing: in his desperate attempt to escape his origins (his low status) he put on airs and graces which convince no-one but himself.

Sometimes a series will have a whole 'pecking order' of statuses, from high to medium to low. *Blackadder* (writers, Richard Curtis, Ben Elton and Rowan Atkinson) works wonderfully in this respect. Each series of *Blackadder* is set in a different period, but the status relationships between the major characters remain a major feature. Blackadder himself is sandwiched between Baldrick, at the bottom of the scale, and the Prince (in the series set vaguely in a sort of Napoleonic period) above him. Each of them speaks in an entirely different way, emphasising their status positions. Baldrick tries to say wise things but only manages idiotic statements; Blackadder speaks in a clipped, precise and measured manner, appropriate to a senior servant of the Prince; and the Prince himself tries to be jolly funny but instead is only jolly silly, but he needn't worry about it as he is a Prince anyway. The status positions of these three characters inform not only the plot but also all of the dialogue. What is particularly hilarious is the inversion of status and how it is handled through the dialogue. Blackadder is the only intelligent one of the three, yet he is always polite. Thus while the Prince is being daft, Blackadder might tell him so (though the Prince rarely understands that this is what Blackadder is doing), but does it while continuing to use polite – courtly – language (further emphasised by Rowan Atkinson's manner of delivery), which in this context is much funnier than outright abuse. Thus Blackadder retains the *language* of his status, and the contradiction between this and the *meaning* of what he is actually saying is a large ingredient of the humour. Then even when Blackadder is speaking to Baldrick it is sometimes in the relatively formal manner appropriate to his station, though in fact he is invariably insulting Baldrick – and much more directly than he does his master. *Again, it is the contrast between what he says and how he says it that produces much of the humour.* Of course, many of the lines are undeniably funny in themselves, but it is the language in the context – and particularly the exploitation of the status element of the context – that is central to the whole comic effect.

Another example of pecking order in comic writing occurs in *Fawlty Towers*, and again the major character is in the middle: Basil Fawlty is pecked by his wife (who to his fury always adopts a position of senior status in relation to him) and in turn pecks Polly and, even more, Manuel. And, again similarly, there is a contrast between the meanings of what the central character says and the language he uses to express them. Very often Fawlty is at the end of his tether, insulting all those around him, but he is constantly battling to try to use appropriate language, and it is this struggle within Fawlty's strangled dialogue which is so extremely funny.

Language and caricature

In some episodes of *Blackadder* the pecking order is further extended, as for example when the character played by Stephen Fry appears. He is a step higher up the status ladder than the Prince. Different series have Fry appear in different roles, though always in the same (high) status position. He is wonderful as the Duke of Wellington, who seems to believe that any army may be disciplined and any battle won if only the generals shout loud enough. The Duke's style of speech, then, is quite distinct from that of the other characters: he shouts, shouts and shouts again.

This leads us to the use of caricature in comic dialogue. There is a delight in believing that generals are pig-headed, caring little either for strategy or for the welfare of those under them, and being content to use brute force (shouting being the verbal equivalent). This is what is being caricatured here. Similarly the language of the Prince is a caricature of that of the upper-class chinless wonder; the language of Blackadder that of the respectful manservant; and the language of Baldrick that of the dumbskull. Certainly each of these is a character in themselves, individual; yet at the same time we recognise them as belonging to type, particularly in their use of language. It is this recognition – despite however absurdly exaggerated the language may be – that greatly adds to our pleasure in listening to them.

In Elizabethan times there was a theory of 'humours'. The word here does not mean comedy, but refers to dominant elements in an individual's character. It was believed that there were four humours, and that when these were properly mixed in someone's personality then that person would be balanced, but if one of them came to dominate then that personality would be unbalanced. Jonson in particular wrote wonderful comedies, such as *Volpone* and *The Alchemist*, full of these unbalanced characters who have allowed themselves to become obsessed by one thing. They may not be fully rounded characters, but they work very well; comedy does not always need fully rounded characters.

Similarly, today, there are many examples of successful comic creation who have little more than one strong characteristic. The dialogue then need not strive for a variety of subtle effects – the recognition of this one characteristic is often enough. In *A Fish Called Wanda* (writers, John Cleese and Charles Crichton), for example, Otto may have other characteristics, but he is also amusingly dominated by his obsessional need not to be called (or thought to be) stupid. In the television series *Red Dwarf*, Cat is even more limited: his dialogue tells us little more than that he is a fashion addict. But we don't complain. In this context, it is enough.

One word of warning on the use of caricature, however: the character must always be *rooted in reality*. I use the term 'caricature' here, but the audience must not be aware of caricature, in the sense of this being a character taken to such an extreme as to be unrecognisable. Caricature when taken this far may be able to raise the odd laugh, but this will not be sustainable; indeed, it may even threaten the credibility of the whole script, as the audience soon ceases to have much interest in a character so far removed from reality as to be beyond recognition.

Character recognition and comic dialogue

Recognition, in fact, plays a significant role in a number of ways in comic dialogue. There is the pleasure of recognition of type of character (we all recognise the type of a grumpy old Victor Meldrew – we have all met one) but there is also recognition of individual character. We have touched upon this in a number of ways already, but now we shall have a closer look at it, referring again to the American series *Friends*.

We noted in the first chapter that Phoebe is continually misreading things: she often attempts to join in a conversation in the same way as the others but just fails to do so. Her unconscious breaking of social codes is, as we noted, both charming and funny. But in addition, every time she says something which just slightly misreads the tone of the conversation, we laugh and say to ourselves, 'She would!' This recognition – that a character in comedy is acting in character – is an important ingredient of the humour. Similarly, when Monica tells someone off for leaving a speck of dust somewhere, or Joey says something particularly inane, the line in itself may not be funny – it would not stand up as 'a joke' – but it may be very funny simply as a result of confirming our view of this character. This 'He would!' or 'She would!' factor should not be underestimated in comic dialogue; it is the humour arising directly from recognition of character trait, *for comic dialogue is utterly intertwined with comic characterisation*. We should not always attempt to write 'funny lines', but should recognise the comic power of the relationship between dialogue and characterisation.

In comic dialogue, then, the characters should not be at the service of the jokes. *Rather, the dialogue should be at the service of the characterisation.*

Laughing at and laughing with

Staying with *Friends* for a while longer, the series also affords an example of the distinction between laughing *with* and laughing *at*. While each of the six regular characters have some lines which they – the speakers – know are funny, only two of the six (Ross and particularly Chandler) are *regularly* allowed to say things which they as characters know are amusing. The humour in the lines of the other four arises almost entirely *despite* the intentions of the character. The character says something which is intended to be taken 'straight' but which we the audience (and often other characters) find funny. To some extent, then, we are laughing *at* the characters rather than *with* them. However, if their faults (and it is usually faults or weakness that we laugh at) are not serious ones, than then the writer can invite the audience to laugh at the characters without diminishing the all-important empathy with them. Once again, we come back to the point that the writer must not try to make the dialogue alone do all the work – in this case in the form of 'jokes'. 'Jokes' arise when characters know they are saying something funny, but we laugh just as much (or, often, more) when a character is not intending to amuse.

Dialogue for one situation as though it were for another

We will use *Friends* to demonstrate a further option for comic scriptwriters: this is writing dialogue for one sort of scene as if it were dialogue for another. For example, when Joey decides to go and get his own apartment, his leaving scene is scripted absolutely as though it were a scene between two lovers splitting up; when Ross and his monkey go to a party and the monkey goes off to have fun without Ross, this too is scripted as though Ross were a jilted lover; when a little boy receives a small bump on the head, the dialogue of the following scene is scripted as though it were from an emergency-ward soap opera. This is all quite sophisticated comic scripting, which calls upon the audience to recognise another type of scene – or even another genre altogether – and to acknowledge that the writer is being playful; it also relies on the characters *not* being aware that there is anything odd going on. Any acknowledgement by the *characters* of what is happening would kill it.

There is something similar at one point in the film *The Mummy Returns* (writers, Stephen Sommers and Lloyd Fonveille). Our heroes are on a London bus that is being ferociously besieged by vile-looking Mummies. Rick is fighting them off valiantly, turning attacker after attacker to dust. But then for one memorable second Rick seems not to find these disgusting creatures a real threat, but rather only a tedious nuisance. 'Mummies!' he says dismissively, bored with them, as he chops another to pieces. We laugh because there is an acknowledgement somewhere here that it is hard for us – the audience – to take all of this too seriously. Rick is reacting to the creatures much as we are: we have seen enough of them attacking the bus like this and want to see a different type of action. The character is almost speaking directly to the audience, but he is not, and the distinction is vital.

Similarly, in one episode of the television series *The New Adventures of Superman*, Perry and Jimmy complain to each other that they are a little irritated that Lois and Clark seem to get all the attention: Perry says it feels as if he and Jimmy were secondary characters in a television series. The humour here is again the knowing wink between writer and audience. If the characters themselves were in on the joke it would cease to be funny. The scriptwriter must take great care in the handling of this sort of irony.

In the examples given so far the technique has been (in different ways) to bypass the knowledge of the character – the joke has gone straight from the writer to the audience without the character knowing it (though in *The Mummy Returns* it is a close thing). This same technique may be extended to a whole script. The entire film *Airplane* (writers, Jim Abrahams, David and Jerry Zucker) is a ludicrous and hilarious pastiche of the serious disaster movie, though of course none of the characters is aware of it. They may be astonished by the staggering ineptitude of Frank Drebin – Leslie Nielsen – but still are unaware of the pastiche nature of what they are part of. The television series *The Detectives* adopts a daft version of cop-show dialogue in order to poke fun at cop shows (as do *Police Squad*, *Naked Gun* and other Nielsen vehicles), while the radio series *People Like Us* is a fake version of a serious radio documentary. In each of these cases the dialogue of the original has clearly been closely observed, then exaggerated and made ridiculous. But, however ludicrous the lines, the scriptwriter must never let the characters in on the joke.

Pathos

The examples we have just been looking at are on the edge of satire, and satire tends not to have great variations of mood. But in much of comedy it is useful also to work into the dialogue an element of pathos. Some comedies – particularly those which tend to be aimed at the lower age-group market – do zip along without any respite from the jokes. If this is the market you decide to aim for, then this is the type of dialogue you need to write. But in general, *humorous dialogue does not have to be funny every moment* – some light and shade is desirable. And strangely, an element of pathos can work not only by acting as a contrast in mood but also by feeding into the humour itself, giving it a particular colour and power. At times *One Foot in the Grave* (writer, David Renwick) almost makes us cry as much as laugh, and this certainly applies to *Steptoe and Son*. Even the series *Absolutely Fabulous* has its sad moments, as these characters, for all their attempts to remain glamorous and to stave off the effects of the years, are funny in part *because* they are rather pathetic. We laugh with them and at them at the same time, and occasionally we are invited not to laugh at all, but just to appreciate the sadness of them. And though a comedy like *Groundhog Day* (writers, Danny

Rubin and Harold Ramis) certainly has some funny lines, the humour of the dialogue is in fact rooted in the *negative* quality of the central character; he is in fact a very sad man (in both modern senses of the word) and while this is a comedy it is at the same time the story of his redemption. Again, it would have been a mistake for the scriptwriter to try to get the dialogue to do all the work of the comedy, in the form of jokes; instead, the pathos feeds the comedy.

Let the situation work

In comic dialogue, as in other forms of dialogue, it is a mistake to try to make the words themselves produce the total comic effect. Characterisation has a large part to play. But so too do other elements. *In film in particular, if there is a choice between making a joke with words or with visuals, always choose the visuals.* (In fact, this piece of advice holds good even when comedy is not involved; in film, visuals should carry as much as possible of the story, and dialogue as little as possible.) Yet again, it is a matter of not making the dialogue work too hard.

Similarly, situations can in themselves be funny, almost without the dialogue. If you describe the situation in *Mrs Doubtfire*, for example (another comedy with plenty of pathos) or *Housesitter*, it is amusing in its own right. The dialogue, then, has to serve the development of this situation. In this sort of comedy, much of the humour is plot-driven, so *while individually funny lines are always welcome, they are less important than lines which feed the humour of the plot.* We have already noted that in comic dialogue the lines should be at the service of the characterisation, and here we note that it must also serve the plot; we are coming to realise that it really is the context which is crucial in allowing the humour itself to surface.

The 'running gag'

The 'running gag' uses repetition to increase the intensity of humour – just as repetition may be used in other forms of dialogue to increase intensity. Basically, there is a joke, usually but not always verbal; the audience laughs. Then each time the joke comes back the audience laughs again, but now they are not just laughing at the joke as in the original, but they are laughing at the fact that whatever it is has actually happened *again* – when usually the character involved should have learned from things the first time round. And they are laughing, too, at their own recognition of the joke. In fact, as soon as it appears that the joke is even *about* to be repeated, the audience starts to laugh.

The running gag can be extremely effective in comic dialogue, but there are dangers as well. The first danger is of monotony. If the gag is simply repeated exactly as in the original, the audience will soon tire of it and it will become not only unfunny but a liability. So there has to be a little variation in how it is expressed, or you have to put the dialogue into a different context. Furthermore, as the audience comes to recognise the gag, less and less needs to be said each time. Eventually it might come down to hardly any words at all. Not only does this allow the gag to continue working, but it adds a further element – the audience enjoys the game of recognising the joke with increasingly fewer clues.

The comic insult

A major ingredient of comic dialogue is the imaginative comic insult. There is enormous variation in these insults. Consider, for example, Basil Fawlty's stream of invective in *Fawlty Towers*, or Blackadder's withering sarcasm, or Harold Steptoe's scornful remarks to his father. We enjoy insults, since they are not normally socially acceptable – these characters are saying what we would love to say on many comparable occasions.

The strength of insults – and thus their comic effect – can be greatly increased by their being repeated back by the recipient. So instead of:

DON: You birdbrain!
NICK: I'm not a birdbrain!

we might prefer:

DON: You birdbrain!
NICK: Birdbrain? *Birdbrain?*

Again, though, the type of insult must be in keeping with the character. One character may totally lose control (Basil Fawlty in one episode both physically and verbally thrashes his *car*), while another may be insulting in a more cool, detached manner. We must not allow ourselves to give rein to an amusing insult if the style fails to fit the character.

Comedy and political correctness

There has been a long debate concerning scriptwriting and political correctness – a debate going back certainly to the first uses of the term itself, and really pre-dating that, though then we spoke of censorship and self-censorship without the specific concept of 'political correctness'. As scriptwriters we all have (and probably always have had) a tendency to censor ourselves, being careful about the language we use: what swear-words should I cut out in order for my script to be seen as acceptable in a given context, and how often may they be used? There is nothing particularly hypocritical in this. We do, after all, moderate our language – or not – in real life, depending upon where we are and whom we are with. Scriptwriting demands that we do the same. The golden rule is: *know your market*. If you are planning to write for children's television, for example, watch it first and see what is generally considered acceptable.

But a scriptwriter should not be too timid. There is a school of thought which suggests that if you think a certain character would swear continually in real life, or a group might indulge in a certain form of unusually deviant sex, or a particular situation would inevitably lead to some horrendous violence, then you should not shrink from showing that in both dialogue and action. Then – or so the argument goes – it is for the commissioning editor, script editor, director or whoever is in the relevant position in whichever medium to decide whether this actually is acceptable or not, and if necessary to make suggestions for alterations (which the scriptwriter may or may not accept). At least then the writer is not doing the censoring.

This is a perfectly reasonable approach, and one which I at least attempt to adopt (though some self-censorship does sometimes creep in nevertheless). But it can have negative consequences. For example, a script with language that is utterly unacceptable for the intended audience might lead a scriptreader to feel that this writer is completely out of touch with both the market and the medium, and thus the script as a whole could be discredited before the writer even has a chance to debate any alterations. The writer should at least be aware of this danger, and then take as much of a risk as they wish in the light of it.

In terms of dialogue, however, the limitations do not only apply to the use of swearing; they also apply to language involving 'political correctness' in general. Thus language that is racist, for example, is (thankfully) almost totally unacceptable unless placed in the mouth of a clearly unsympathetic character. But other issues are much greyer, and these touch upon comic dialogue even more frequently than upon other forms.

Should we as scriptwriters feel inhibited from portraying negatively any of our female characters, or any black characters, or disabled ones? There is no easy answer. Certainly we would not wish to contribute to caricatured ideas of foreigners, or the general belittling of women... but if we are not to allow our dialogue to portray *any* women, blacks or foreigners in a negative light, surely we end up writing in a strait-jacket; we finish up, in fact, with another set of caricatures – the politically correct set. And this set of characters to which we find ourselves limited simply cannot fulfil the needs of drama, as they cannot speak or act as people actually do speak or act, and thus the audience cannot relate to them, so little good is done anyway. The scriptwriter, then, has to attempt to balance the legitimate demand that we should not malign groups of people with the demand that we should represent people as they are – and perhaps show how they may change.

Comic dialogue likes to be honest. If it shows two men – or two women for that matter – discussing someone of the opposite sex, and then dismissing that person as a partner because they are too tall, short, fat, thin or whatever, this may be entirely politically incorrect but we laugh because we recognise it. We think, 'Yes, exactly!'; whether or not we approve, we may well still find it funny. After all, there are many things we do ourselves which we do not approve of – we might even be a little ashamed of them – but we recognise them when they are portrayed in front of us. It is no use the scriptwriter presenting a sanitised world. As I have emphasised already, a major element in effective comic dialogue is recognition, so comic dialogue needs to show us what we recognise – and this includes the politically incorrect. (Saints tend not to be very amusing, not just because they don't say funny lines but also because most of us don't know any saints – we don't recognise them. *But people who want to be seen as saints are amusing*, partly because they say funny lines – often without knowing it – and also because we recognise them: we all know people who *want* to be considered saints.)

So a series like *Till Death Us Do Part* (writer, Johnny Speight) shows a whole set of dreadful attitudes, mostly displayed by a character who is clearly bigoted and – literally – ignorant. We all know people with these attitudes, and here we have these attitudes presented for us to laugh at. Similarly, *Men Behaving Badly* (writer, Simon Nye) shows men doing just that: these are lager-swilling oafs, and though they may be soft at heart they nevertheless display appalling attitudes towards society in general and women in particular. Again, we recognise them and are invited to laugh at them (though without losing all empathy).

But there is a danger here, of which the scriptwriter should be aware. However we are meant to regard *Till Death Us Do Part*, it is possible that some racists may feel *supported* by the portrayal of Alf Garnett. He is a figure to be ridiculed, but this is not the reaction of everyone. Similarly, there may well be a section of viewers watching *Men Behaving Badly* who – even if at the same time as laughing – feel that some of their own attitudes towards women are vindicated by these men, who despite everything are essentially sympathetic characters. What a scriptwriter might present to an audience with a certain ironic approach might in fact be taken literally, at least by some viewers.

So the scriptwriter ought to be aware of this danger, which tends to arise particularly in comedy. We want comic dialogue to deal with taboos, with serious issues, to poke fun, but it may be misinterpreted. Perhaps the risk is worth taking. Perhaps even to worry about it is to be, to some extent, patronising. But whatever attitude we take towards it, the risk certainly exists.

11. Documentary Dialogue

What is documentary dialogue?

Up to this point this book has been looking at the writing of dialogue in scripts which are essentially dealing in fiction. Some plays and films are based upon factual events, but usually the dialogue is fictional, even if a few factual speeches are included. This chapter, however, deals with dialogue of a very specific nature, for documentary drama.

The term 'documentary drama' covers a very wide spectrum. At one extreme it simply means a play or film (or what for radio or television is sometimes called a 'dramatised feature') closely based upon real events. In this type of production, while the plot will keep as closely as possible to known facts, the dialogue will be at least in part – and usually to a very large extent – fictional. Sometimes this form is referred to as 'faction', the mixture of fact and fiction.

There have been some interesting recent developments in the dialogue of 'faction'. In my own radio script *Everything Will Be Fine*, for example, most of the voices we hear are the actual voices of taped interviewees telling of their experiences as refugees. Within this there are two voices that we as listeners assume are also 'actuality' but are in fact the voices of actors speaking scripted dialogue. This only becomes clear after about half an hour of the programme, as little by little the story-telling spreads out to become a re-enactment of events, so that we become aware that we must be hearing (at least some) actors. The questions then become: how do we know which interviewees have been actors? How do we judge who is telling the truth? At the same time, the fact that the long and (apparently) purely documentary opening section has allowed us to believe that we are hearing 'reality' lends a certain credibility to the re-enactments which then arise out of that section. At any rate, the initial misleading of the audience points up the strained relationship between documentaries and reality: as documentaries commissioned by the Third Reich demonstrate, the fact that something is a documentary does not mean that it is presenting the truth.

At the other extreme from the true story with fictionalised dialogue, the term 'documentary drama' can be interpreted to mean a play or film in which not only did all the events occur in reality, but also almost everything spoken is documentary as well – the *exact* words coming either from tape-recorded and transcribed interviews or from written sources such as letters, reports, council minutes, newspapers, official records or school logs. With minimal alterations and very few additions, the words from the source or a variety of sources are knitted together rather like a patchwork, to form a drama. This is very different from the other, less strict, version of the form. Then there is also the huge range of documentary drama which falls between these two extremes.

Leaving aside the experimental use of faction as in *Everything Will Be Fine*, the first extreme differs relatively little, in terms of dialogue, from a well-researched fiction-based script. Of course the dialogue is limited in that it should not stray from what is already known about the real characters (and remember, real characters, if still alive, can certainly bite back if they believe that they are being defamed!), but otherwise all that has been said in earlier chapters applies. The purpose of this chapter, however, is to look at the techniques involved in writing dialogue closer to the second extreme, which is *strictly* documentary drama.

Before we move on to do so, however, we should briefly answer the following question: why should any scriptwriter bother to work in such a constricting form as strict documentary drama? There are two main reasons. First, the language from original source materials is often quite wonderful, and its preservation in a script can really lift it. Second, and more important, keeping almost entirely to the exact words adds tremendous authenticity to a script. Of course, any script is still the subjective work of the author; but it does make a difference if a writer can tell the audience that the words they have heard have almost all been said or written by the people concerned. This applies particularly in the flourishing world of community theatre.

From interview to dialogue

Let us say that the following is a tape-recorded interview which has been transcribed; we will look at the ways in which it might be transformed into dialogue.

MIKE: Well I'll tell you about... let me tell you about this particular day. This particular day we'd all been got into assembly. And in those days of course you couldn't come in chatting or any of that – you had to come in in single file, and you'd all be standing up straight and not saying a word, 'cause that's how it was in those days, not like it is now. So anyway, I can see it now, there we all were, standing up straight, and then when we were told to sit we'd all sit down, but on the floor, we'd sit on the floor with our legs crossed, 'cause there wasn't enough chairs in the hall for the whole school, or maybe there was, I don't know, but anyway we sat down in the hall. And the Headmaster, he was up the front and the teachers were all the way round, and usually, but not today for some reason... Normally he'd just give some little talk – you know, some homily, and that's what – some little story, and then a prayer, and then he'd give some notices – like not to walk on a particular bit of grass or whatever. Whatever seemed important. But today he took it into his head, instead of saying the Lord's Prayer like he always did with us joining in – 'Our Father, which art in heaven...' – but instead of this, he says, 'Paul, come here, and you can recite the Lord's Prayer.' Why he picked on this boy Paul I've no idea, but anyway he did, so Paul looks shocked – remember we were only about nine or ten – 'Come on, stand up, come to the front.' So Paul goes to the front and – maybe the Head thought it'd be really nice to have a boy recite the Lord's Prayer instead of him saying it. Goes to the front. Maybe he thought it'd, I don't know, make it seem more real or something. I don't know. So anyway, this boy Paul starts to recite the Lord's Prayer, and of course he's shaking. He's in front of the whole school and the Headmaster's breathing there in front of him, and you could see he's shaking. And he can't keep it up. He gets as far as 'Forgive us our trespasses...' and then he says it again, 'Forgive us our trespasses...' and that's as far as he can get.

And the Head just stares at him. He does a little nod, like to say – Yes? Yes? but Paul's gone. He's blank. And there's this horrible silence, everyone waiting for something to happen. But nothing does. So then the Head, he goes to his briefcase, big old leather briefcase, and he takes out his ruler, and then he gets hold of Paul's hand and he lifts it up and sort of flattens it out. He gives him three wacks of the ruler – one, two, three, and Paul bursts into tears but the Head just says to him, 'Sit down' and then he turns to the rest of the school and says, 'You will all learn the Lord's Prayer.' And I've never forgotten it. Not the Lord's Prayer I mean, but that day. And it taught me everything I've ever wanted to know about religion – well, organised religion – and about tyranny too. I've never forgotten it.

So, how might this be reworked into dialogue for the stage? Already, as a piece of story-telling it is very effective, but it will need to be reworked in some ways in order to function well on the stage. Here is one version:

MICHAEL: (*to audience*) It taught me everything I've ever wanted to know about religion.
School children, including MICHAEL, are coming in, single file, standing up straight, while teachers take their places round the outside of the space, the Headmaster at the front. Two children very quietly exchange a word.
TEACHER: You two!
The two children are instantly silent.
2nd TEACHER: (*to two other children*) Up straight!
All the children are now present. After a couple of seconds of silence –
HEADMASTER: Sit down.
All children sit cross-legged on the floor.
MICHAEL: (*to audience*) Normally he'd just give some little talk – you know, some homily, some little story – and then a prayer, and then he'd give some notices – like not to walk on a particular bit of grass or whatever. Whatever seemed important. But today he took it into his head, instead of saying the Lord's Prayer like he always did with us joining in –
HEADMASTER: Paul, come here.

Clearly shocked, PAUL, one of the children, looks around to check it really is him the Headmaster wants.

MICHAEL: (*to audience*) Why he picked on this boy Paul I've no idea.

HEADMASTER: Come on, stand up, come to the front.

While PAUL makes his way to the front –

MICHAEL: Maybe he thought it'd be really nice –

HEADMASTER: You can recite the Lord's Prayer.

MICHAEL: – to have a boy recite it.

Pause, as all wait for PAUL to speak.

PAUL: Our Father, which art in Heaven, Hallow'd be thy name, Thy Kingdom come, Thy will be done, on Earth as it is in Heaven, Give us this day our daily bread... and forgive us our trespasses... and forgive us our trespasses...

PAUL has frozen. Everyone waits.

The HEADMASTER goes to his old leather briefcase, takes out a ruler, then gestures to Paul to hold his hand out. He makes sure Paul's hand is suitably open, then brings the ruler down on Paul's hands three times. Paul bursts into tears.

HEADMASTER: Sit down.

As PAUL returns to his place –

HEADMASTER: You will all learn the Lord's Prayer.

MICHAEL: Everything I've ever wanted to know about religion – well, organised religion – and about tyranny too. I've never forgotten it.

The process here is relatively simple. There has been some editing of the original interview speech, and one line – 'Everything I've ever wanted to know about religion' – has been repeated, but the quality of the actual speech has for the most part been retained. The most important point to note is that *as much as possible has in fact been taken out of speech and put into action,* and as much as possible of what is left in speech has been given to other characters and shown rather than merely *told.* It should also be noted that *duplication has been avoided*: you either show something or you tell the audience about it. If you are consciously aiming for a very specific effect, such as a comic one, the combination of both showing and telling can have a humorous effect as in the following example:

GEORGE: (*to audience*) So she bonked him over the head.
    SARAH hits BARRY over the head with a box file.
GEORGE: (*to audience*) And it hurt.
BARRY: Oy! That hurt!

Usually, however, you should do one or the other.

Stylised documentary dialogue

In the above example about the Lord's Prayer, the taped speech from one person has been split up between a number of speakers. This often happens in documentary drama. Now let us take the following as part of an interview:

JILL: We were going like the clappers in this beaten-up old thing, I don't think it had ever done this speed in its life before, and Cherry had got her head out the window yelling at all the passers-by and Sheila and Penny were in the back shouting things like 'Is this all it can do?' 'Put your foot down' – but my foot was flat on the floor as it was, I mean we were determined to get to the cinema before the thing started and, well it was fun too, I mean it felt really great... all of us together... And then – well you know this – the tyre blew, the front tyre on the driver's side, and there wasn't time to say anything, not even... well I mean maybe someone said 'Oh God' or something but I don't remember any screaming, though there may have been, I think we just sort of clung on – to whatever – just sort of clung on, and first we went all over the road and then we went off into this ditch and you could feel the balance going and we went over, and over, and over, and then we stopped. I thought I'd had it. I thought we all had. And then there was a moment, well I say a moment, I don't know how long it was – but thinking, 'I'm still alive. I'm still here.' And then we all started checking that we were all there. And we were, God knows how, especially Cherry, who'd had her head out the window. She was in hospital for three months, traction, on her back, but she was alive. The front window, the windscreen, it came out in one piece – I suppose it's meant to do that, and we all crawled out of that. We didn't deserve to be alive, I suppose.

Now let's see how this might be presented in a documentary stage play:

> *JILL, CHERRY, PENNY and SHEILA face the audience.*

SHEILA: The front window, the windscreen, it came out in one piece – I suppose it's meant to do that, and we all crawled out of that.

> *JILL, CHERRY, PENNY and SHEILA take up positions as though in car. JILL is driving, SHEILA has her head out of the window and SHEILA and PENNY are in the back. They are all obviously enjoying themselves.*

JILL: (*yell – as though over the sound of the engine*) We –

PENNY: (*yell*) – were –

SHEILA: (*yell*) – going –

JILL: Like the clappers!

PENNY: – in this beaten-up old thing.

SHEILA: I don't think it had ever done this speed in its life before, and Cherry –

CHERRY: Yoohoo!!

SHEILA: – had got her head out the window.

PENNY: (*to JILL*) Is this all it can do?

SHEILA: (*to JILL*) Put your foot down!

JILL: It's flat on the floor as it is!

CHERRY: We're going to get there before it starts!

SHEILA: And it was fun.

JILL: It felt great!

PENNY: All of us together!

> *All freeze. This is held for a few moments, and then while the others stay frozen SHEILA turns to us.*

SHEILA: I don't remember any screaming, though there may have been.

> Someone may have said 'Oh God.'

> A tyre'd blown.

> We just sort of clung on.

> *PENNY and JILL slowly turn to us, but CHERRY remains frozen.*

PENNY: Sort of clung on...

JILL: Clung on to...

SHEILA: Clung on to whatever.

> *Now suddenly all, including CHERRY, are totally unfrozen,*

and screaming, as together they turn over and over.
All lie still, silent.
JILL: And I thought, 'I'm still alive. I'm still here.'
  (*slight pause*)
  You there?
PENNY: Yeah.
SHEILA: Yeah.
  (*slight pause*)
JILL: Cherry?
  (*slight pause*)
SHEILA: Cherry was still there, God knows how.
CHERRY: I was in hospital for three months, traction, on my back. But I was alive.

Here, as in the previous example, we have one original speech distributed over a number of characters, though this time there are a great many more changes in sentence order than in the previous one. The major difference, though, is that this time the style of the dialogue – while remaining as faithful to the original – is much less naturalistic. The transformation of the opening sentence into a series of yells conveys the excitement and exuberance of that moment, along with the feeling that this was very much a *shared* experience – they even share this utterance (a technique, as we have seen, also available in other non-documentary but highly stylised dialogue). Of course in real life four women would never divide a sentence up between them like this, but this is theatrical dialogue, not real life. Then:

  ... We just sort of clung on.
  PENNY and JILL slowly turn to us, but CHERRY remains frozen.
PENNY: Sort of clung on...
JILL: Clung on to...
SHEILA: Clung on to whatever.

– again emphasises, through the shared words and the painfully slow progress through the phrase, both that this was a very difficult experience to cope with and, once more, that it was shared between them. The non-naturalism of the dialogue matches the non-naturalism of the visual presentation.

The material is divided up almost entirely between three of the four characters. Some of the lines of narration could easily have been given to Cherry, but by not giving her lines of narration (until the very end) we place her somehow outside of the memory, and this seems to imply that she did not survive, particularly given that she had had her head out of the window. This heightens the tension, though at the end, when she speaks to the audience for the first time, we discover that she did live after all.

In the original, taped interview we are told of the tyre-burst when it happens. In the new version this information is fed into the dialogue differently. First, at the start, we are told that they had crawled out of the windscreen, which had come out in one piece. This adds an edge to the section immediately following, where the characters are all full of high spirits but we know something dreadful is going to happen. Then when the tyre blows we are not told immediately. Instead we are given:

> *All freeze. This is held for a few moments, and then while the others stay frozen SHEILA turns to us.*
>
> SHEILA: I don't remember any screaming, though there may have been.
> Someone may have said 'Oh God.'
> A tyre'd blown.
> We just sort of clung on.

Here there is a slight jump in time, Sheila first telling us how she and the other women did or did not react. This too increases the tension – react to what? Only then does she tell us.

So, to summarise, the scriptwriter:

- presents a mixture of characters narrating and speaking to each other;
- alters the timing of the release of information;
- maximises tension;
- divides the lines non-naturalistically to emphasise meaning;
- transforms much of the original into action (which is also non-naturalistic);
- takes great care over duplication of telling/showing.

Dialogue pieced together

So far, we have looked at how individual speeches – personal anecdotes – may be scripted for a number of characters. However, documentary material may not be anecdotal in the first place, but rather may take the form of a number of fragments. In this case the process is something like the reverse of the above. For example, in amongst the research material may be the following fragments:

1) from school log:
   20th May.
   Again many boys absent, believed to be at Mr Hammond's brickworks. Some have not been seen for weeks now. I have written to Mr Hammond to request that we meet to discuss the situation.

2) from a taped interview:
   Of course, we'd be working down the brickfields all summer, whether we was meant to be at school or not. That's how I got my first job as a barrow boy down at Hammond's, from having worked there on and off since I was twelve. It brought a bit of extra money into the house, didn't it?

3) from a book about brick-making before the First World War:
   The barrow boy would bring the pug to the pug mill ready for the moulder. The moulder, who was himself on top wages, would be in charge of his gang, or 'stool', and would be responsible for paying them, except for the barrow boy, who would receive his money separately.

These three fragments might then be welded into a single scene or a mini-sequence of scenes, as follows:

The MOULDER is at work, shaping bricks.
MOULDER: Right, you bring the pug to the pug mill, for me. I'm the moulder.
BOY Right.

Separately, a TEACHER approaches the HEADTEACHER.
TEACHER: There are many boys absent again.

HEADTEACHER: And where –
TEACHER: I believe they are at Mr Hammond's brickworks.

Back to the brickworks:
BOY: (*to audience*) That's how I got my first job down at Hammond's –
MOULDER: I'm in charge of the stool.
BOY: (*to audience*) – from working there on and off since I was twelve.
MOULDER: And I'm responsible for paying them. Except you. You get yours separately.

Back at the school:
TEACHER: Some have not been seen for weeks now.
HEADTEACHER: Well then, I shall write to Mr Hammond, requesting that we meet to discuss the situation.

At the brickworks:
BOY: It brought a bit of extra money into the house didn't it?

The source material has here been spliced together to produce a sequence which works, material from two of the sources being used together in one location while the school log extract is used as a counterpoint – we see the educationalists' attitude at the same time as we see the boy's pride in what he achieved.

This example does lead us to the problem of mixing written and verbal sources within documentary drama. Occasionally, where a word from a written document seems too inappropriate for dialogue, it will be changed (as above, 'You get yours separately' as opposed to 'received' in the original), but mostly it is best to keep to the source version. An audience comes to realise that, as this is documentary drama, the dialogue will not always work exactly as in other forms, and while much of the language will be wonderfully believable – it has, after all, been transcribed verbatim from someone speaking – other parts will have a certain stilted quality. Indeed, very often it is possible to draw attention to the fact that the original was written rather than verbal – sometimes Council Minutes will include, in the playscript itself, 'It was agreed that...' or a letter might include the date and address.

The challenge of documentary dialogue

Dialogue in documentary drama can be as exciting as in any other form, though the challenges for the scriptwriter are somewhat different. There is a basic limitation: you must stay as close as you feel is possible to the exact words from the sources, and this is difficult. On the other hand, this limitation can prove a blessing in disguise, as it often forces the scriptwriter to find more imaginative ways of presenting material (visual or musical, perhaps), as dialogue cannot merely be made up as it normally could be. The documentary form invites us into a non-naturalistic presentation of dialogue which otherwise simply might not occur to us.

One last word on documentary dialogue. There are certain tricks of the trade which the scriptwriter will quite rightly use, such as putting a speech from one original source into the mouths of a number of characters, or for that matter putting the speeches from a number of sources into the mouth of one character. The scriptwriter has to be sensitive, and never have any *named and identifiable character* (as opposed to, say, 1st Labourer or 2nd Milliner) speak a line which was not theirs originally and which they would object to having attributed to them. This means that contributors should, where appropriate, have the opportunity to point out where a line seems false. In practice there are very rarely any problems, *as long as the scriptwriter is true not only as far as possible to the letter of the sources, but also to the spirit of them.* After all, as any news editor will confirm, it is perfectly possible to quote nothing but what was actually said, yet to select and present the quotes in such a way as to put forward something a very long way from the real truth. Documentary drama is just the same, and as it carries the name 'documentary' – referring to the dialogue more than anything – the responsibility upon the scriptwriter to be true to the spirit of the material is greater than ever.

12. How it Looks on the Page

The importance of presentation

How you present your dialogue is important. Scruffy presentation, or a layout which shows complete ignorance of the usual conventions, can be extremely off-putting for a scriptreader (and the term 'scriptreader' here embraces directors and producers). You need to convey an impression of professionalism.

In this book I have presented quotations in a number of different formats, even where the material has been written for the same medium. This has been to demonstrate that, while there are certainly general conventions, there are no absolutely hard and fast rules. The truth is that if a script is presented *clearly*, then even if it does not meet the precise layout expectations of the reader it will probably receive a fair reading. All of the presentation styles used in this book – and others – are acceptable, except that for reasons of space I have not followed the usual convention of having doubled the space between speeches.

Before we come to the specific layout conventions for each of the various media, though, let us look once more at the presentation of simultaneous speech, overlappings and interruptions, and then at 'stage directions' (the term is used for theatre and other media) to actors. You might wish to turn again to page 8, the extract from *Top Girls*, which gives one clearly thought-out example of how you could to present various forms of simultaneous speech. More often, though, scriptwriters tend simply to put before the relevant speech '*simultaneous with SHEILA's speech*', '*simultaneous with the above, starting at...*', '*overlapping*', '*cutting in*', '*interrupting*' or '*continuing without a break*'. The end of an interrupted speech is sometime marked ' – ' and sometimes '...', but the three dots are also often used to denote a speech which trails away, or hesitation, so although there are no clear rules here it is probably best to reserve the dash at the end of a speech for being interrupted, and then a dash at the beginning of a speech means continuing after interruption.

Stage directions for actors

There are two types of stage directions: those for director and crew, and those for the actors. We shall look at the first type later, but here we shall deal with stage directions for the performers. The general advice is, *use them as sparingly as possible.*

The writer must not try to do everything. The writer writes the lines, but it is the actor's job to deliver them, and it is part of the director's job to advise on that delivery. The writer makes a serious mistake if he or she tries to take over these jobs. First, both actor and director will begin to feel insulted by being told how to deliver each line; and second, if they were to follow such instructions (and they almost certainly wouldn't anyway!) then the production would be denied two extra layers of creativity.

If a scene is well written, actors will be able to *feel* how to deliver the lines. Both the text and the sub-text – the meanings running beneath the actual words – will lead the actors and directors to present the dialogue in a certain way. *But this way is not fixed, and it is a mistake for a writer to try to fix it.* Think of the multitude of interpretations given to, say, *Hamlet,* and you will realise that to try to pin down the performers is an error. There is not one 'right' interpretation, but rather many different ways of looking at the material. Yet many inexperienced writers pepper their scripts with directions to the actors – *'quietly', 'with feeling', 'absolutely furious', 'wanting to express the full force of his emotion, yet restraining himself, though we can feel his bitterness nevertheless'.*

The occasional stage direction to an actor is perfectly accept-able, but when given on every other line it seems to imply a lack of confidence on the part of the scriptwriter, as though he or she is not sure that the lines stand up on their own. In general, stage directions to actors should be used only when the meaning is contrary to what the line would normally suggest, for example:

PAUL: (*with affection*) Get out!

Successful scriptwriters vary in their approach to stage directions for actors, but if you turn again to the extracts from *Restoration* (page 118), *Top Girls* (page 8), *The Bill* (pp. 48–9), *A Few Kind Words* (pp. 106–8) and *The English Patient* (pp. 73–4) you will find no stage directions for actors at all in the first two examples. In the extract from *The Bill*, there are a host of directions to the actors but with only one exception these are technical, not about the way the lines should be delivered in terms of feeling (the one exception is the underlining in the line 'She's <u>my body</u>'). Similarly in the extract from *A Few Kind Words* there is only one instruction stating how a line should be delivered, while in *The English Patient* there are just two (plus others dealing with gesture). As you can see, then, in whatever medium, stage directions to actors are generally used sparingly. Incidentally, this has a further added benefit: the fewer stage directions are given, the more those which *are* given will be likely to be followed.

Now let us move on to the layout.

General rules for layout

While there are differences in layout of dialogue for each of the media, there are some rules which apply to all media.

- *Write on A4 paper, using one side only.*
- *Always type or word-process. Never present a hand-written script.*
- *Distinguish clearly between speech and stage directions.*
- *In stage directions, always refer to characters in the same way. Do not, for example, refer to a character by surname at one point, and then by first name later, and never shorten to mere initials.*
- *Always present a neat, clean and corrected script (without, of course, the corrections showing!).*

Apart from the advice given below for presentation of dialogue for each of the script media, other suggestions outside the scope of this book (as they deal with matters other than dialogue) are available. *Writers' and Artists' Yearbook* (A & C Black) is an extremely useful starting point, and as well as the guidelines it contains it goes on to make further recommendations for reading, such as Gerald Kelsey's *Writing for Television* (A & C Black), *The Way to Write for Television* (Elm Tree Books) and *Writing Comedy* by Ronald Wolfe

(Hale). The article *Screenplay for Films* by Jean McDonnell, also in *Writers' and Artists' Yearbook*, gives helpful advice, and I would also suggest that those interested in writing for radio contact the BBC for a (free) copy of the leaflet *Writing Plays for Radio*. The BBC also makes available a set of guidelines (and opportunities) for prospective television scriptwriters.

Layout for radio dialogue

The layout recommended in the BBC leaflet is that lines should be single-spaced, with an extra space left between speeches. In fact when the scripts are typed up by the BBC the spacing is usually 1½-space or double, as this is easier for actors to read, so it seems sensible to type in this format from the start (I use 1½).

The names of speakers go in the left-hand margin, and nothing else goes in this margin. These names and all stage directions (other than directions to actors on how to deliver the lines) go in upper-case letters; all the dialogue and directions to actors on how to deliver the lines (which go in parenthesis) are in the normal 'sentence case' (as opposed to upper-case). Stage directions may be indented further than the dialogue. This may sound complicated, but it is very straightforward. So, while it is perfectly respectable to present a script as it looks on page 106, an example of officially recommended format would look like this:

> (OUTDOORS. SOUNDS AS FOR A STATION.)
> STEVE: I'm not at all sure about this.
> PENNY: Why on earth not? You said you wanted to go. You said you'd always wanted to go. So what's the problem?
> (A HIGH-SPEED TRAIN APPROACHES, THEN RUSHES THROUGH THE STATION.)
> STEVE: (struggling to be heard) The problem... The problem... is that I didn't mean you to take me seriously.
> PENNY: What?

Dialogue layout for the stage

Dialogue layout for the stage is in fact very similar to that for radio, but whereas for radio there is in this country one dominant market – the BBC – which is therefore in a position to dictate a particular format, this is not the case for stage writing.

The most common format is as for the above radio example, except that the directions in upper case would be altered to normal mixed ('sentence') case and would instead be italicised, as would the directions to actors. Characters' names mentioned in stage directions remain in upper case. Sometimes, too, the dialogue is allowed to come back into the margin which is also used for the speakers' names.

In recent years some stage writers have adopted the format associated with film writing, with the speaker's name in the middle of the page (an example of film format is given below). While this is acceptable, the more conventional, non-centred, layout for theatre writing is still more common.

Dialogue layout for film

A full description and analysis of screenplay presentation is available from a number of sources. Apart from those already mentioned these include Robert A. Berman's *Fade In: The Screenwriting Process* (Michael Wiese Film Productions) and *Teach Yourself Screenwriting*, by Raymond G. Frensham (Hodder and Stoughton). Here I shall limit myself just to the dialogue itself.

Again, there is no precise agreement between various writers and production companies, but there is general accord that the speaker's name is placed in upper case in the centre of the page, and then the dialogue, in normal sentence case, immediately below it. There are margins on each side of the page, and of the part of the page which is used the dialogue takes about half the width, a central block (though each line is not actually centred). While scene headings are in upper case, stage directions are in normal sentence case, and use the full width apart from the margins. Character names mentioned in stage directions are always in upper case. Where there are stage directions for the actor rather than the director, these go centrally too (but again not actually centred) but in a narrow band, only about half the width used by the dialogue.

Again, this sounds much more complicated than it is. It is perfectly clear when seen on the page:

INT. KITCHEN, JENNY'S HOUSE. DAY.

JENNY is rushing round preparing a complicated meal, while PAUL sits on a stool.

PAUL

So then that little creep Brewer came up and said that the deadline had been yesterday, so I'd missed it.

JENNY

What?

PAUL

So I told him –

JENNY

(slipping with the knife and cutting her finger)
Blast!

PAUL

I said, 'No it's not until Friday.'

JENNY

I've cut myself!

PAUL

It wasn't true of course.

JENNY

Get me a plaster.

PAUL

What?

JENNY

A plaster! I'm dripping blood!

PAUL finally gets off his stool and goes to a cupboard.

Dialogue layout for television

Many television scripts have to be presented in film format, as they are actually made on film. These include television films of course, but also mini-series and some one-off scripts. Otherwise, the scripts which are produced in the studio or on tape should be presented in television format. Again, there are books such as Kelsey's *Writing for Television* which give the details of every aspect of television-script presentation (indicating different sorts of shots, etc.), but here we are restricting ourselves to the dialogue.

In television format, the scriptwriter uses only the right-hand two-thirds of the page, (except for scene headings, which in some versions of this format go right across the page). This is in order to leave the left-hand side free for additions by the director and production team. Apart from this, the script as presented would be precisely as shown in the extract from *The Bill* on pages 48–9, so part of it would look like this:

13. EXT. STATION FORECOURT. DAY. 9.08AM

FROM OPPOSITE DIRECTIONS THE PANDA CAR AND AREA CAR ARRIVE. THEY BOTH STOP, THOUGH THE AREA CAR SWERVES TO BLOCK THE ALLEY EXIT. ALL FOUR OFFICERS GET OUT (STAMP AND DATTA FROM THE AREA CAR, QUINNAN AND FORD FROM THE PANDA CAR) AND AS THEY DO SO THE WOMAN COMES RUNNING FROM THE WASTEGROUND. SHE VIRTUALLY RUNS STRAIGHT INTO STAMP'S ARMS.

STAMP: (TO FORD AND QUINNAN, WHILE HOLDING ON TO THE WOMAN) What kept you? (TO WOMAN) You're nicked. What's your name?

NOW ALL AT THE SAME TIME FORD IS TALKING TO QUINNAN, STAMP IS CAUTIONING THE WOMAN AND DATTA IS SPEAKING INTO HER RADIO. WE FIND OURSELVES CLOSEST TO FORD AND QUINNAN. BEHIND ALL THIS WE SEE STRINGER ARRIVE, BREATHLESS.

FORD: What goes in must come out, eh?
QUINNAN: Yeah, well I didn't say where, did I?
DATTA: (SIMULTANEOUS WITH THE ABOVE) (INTO RADIO) Sierra Oscar from 181, receiving?

As in the other media, the details of the preferred format presentation will vary from one production company to another – and even from one series to another – but the basic principles remain the same.

A word of warning

Dialogue should never be presented sloppily. It is not difficult to write in the various formats, and after a while each of them can become almost second nature. But sometimes when giving workshops for aspiring writers I find they want me to give disproportionate attention to the minutiae of presentation. It is important, of course, but while poor presentation may damage your chances of a fair reading, a perfect-looking script cannot compensate for poor dialogue – it is still the quality of the writing itself that really counts.

13. Reworking the Dialogue

The need for rewrites

The point was made in an earlier chapter that a certain amount of rewriting of dialogue should be done as you go along. You read through the work of the previous session, making whatever alterations seem necessary, before plunging into the next part. But in this chapter we will look at the rewriting which takes place later, when the initial draft is complete.

The most important point to make is that the first draft really *is* only a first draft. There is a terrible temptation, when you have finally written the last scene, to think, 'Great! That's it! All done!', stick it in an envelope, post it and hope for the best. It is as if it were a baby, and now that it has finally been born you are determined that it should not be mutilated. (Some writers also make the similar mistake of refusing to allow script editors, producers, directors or actors to have any effect upon the script.) Such an approach is fatal. *A first draft always benefits from rewriting.* The rewrites may be quite drastic, affecting fundamental points of plot or setting, but whether or not other major elements are involved, there is always rewriting of the dialogue to be done.

Give it time

Always wait at least a few weeks before rewriting, and longer if at all possible. Of course, there may be occasions on which you are hard up against a deadline and so realise that it is not possible to put the script aside before returning to it – but that is all the more reason not to find yourself in this position. (We have all done it, of course – but our writing has suffered as a result.) You should always plan your writing to allow for this time gap as well as for the rewriting itself. This period is needed because when the script is very fresh in the memory it is virtually impossible to read it as others would who are not acquainted with it. When you go back to your script you want to be as close as you possibly can to reading it as though for the first time. Of course you can't *actually* be reading it as though for the first time – you wrote it, after all! – but the longer you leave it before returning to it, the better. You will want to feel as a scriptreader might feel on being presented with this new product: does the structure work; is a certain surprise in the plot convincing; are the climaxes correctly placed; is the use of time appropriate? And above all you want to *feel* – both in an overall sense and line by line – whether the dialogue works.

It is probably best to read the whole script through at one sitting first, just jotting down notes very quickly but not stopping to deal with every tiny point. This way the overall effect of the dialogue (and other aspects of the writing) becomes clear: you get some idea of whether or not you are generally on the right track. Then it is time for the more thorough reading.

Incidentally, if, like most scriptwriters, you work straight on to computer, it is best to print off the script and read it from that rather than from the screen. Simple typing errors (*not* always detected by a spell-check) seem to go unnoticed on the screen but not on the page, and the whole feel of reading a script – with luck, lying back and enjoying it – is quite different. And this is how the scriptreader will approach it, too.

So, looking at the dialogue with a genuine openness and willingness to rewrite, what should you be looking out for?

Every line must pay its way

However right a line may have felt when you first committed it to the page, now it has to justify itself: you have to be hard-headed. Every line must pay its way. Of course, the payments will vary enormously. Some lines will contribute mostly to plot, some to characterisation, some to comic effect, some to motivation. Some will imply sub-text, some will build up tension. Some will be there as wallpaper – but a wallpaper that is *saying* something. *But any lines which do not pay their way – however 'realistic' in the sense that this might well be what people would actually say – must go.* You must be willing to cut even the lines you most like in themselves, if they are contributing nothing to your script. There is no such thing as a neutral line; *a line is either for you or against you.* It is either contributing positively, or it is merely holding things up. Be brutal.

Check that you are not using dialogue to feed information to the audience. Remember that *for a line to be said there must be a need on the part of the character to say it.* Your need to tell the audience something is not enough. Which brings us on to motivation. Every individual line must have a credible motivation, whether conscious or unconscious, and the overall motivations of each of the characters – what comes out through their dialogue (and actions) through the course of the script – must be coherent and credible. Be certain that the motivation is clear rather than vague, and on the other hand that it is not crudely or unsubtly expressed.

Check that you have not written dialogue that is too literal. *Make sure that there really are sub-texts and agendas operating through every passage.* Check that the dialogue isn't simply superficial, but involves *genuine interaction between characters.*

Cut conversational ping-pong.

Make sure that the dialogue is not taking all the mystery out of the plot by giving information too early, or *the mystery out of characterisation* by making statements that are too clear. (There may be moments when your characters will declare very clearly their motivations or beliefs, or what they think is the kernel of a conflict; it is only if this is happening continually that you need to start wielding the knife.)

In short, check that your dialogue is leaving enough work for the audience to do.

Cut clichés.

Make sure that *the dialogue has enough variation of pace.* Alter it if it is too slow or static; also alter it if it is unremittingly fast and frantic. Similarly, check that there is *enough variation of tone of dialogue,* both within scenes and between them.

Cut out any padding. (Naturally, you didn't think it was padding when you wrote it, but now you can see that it is.) Don't let dialogue ramble. *Try to shorten the dialogue in scenes, particularly beginnings and endings.*

Be sure that *your dialogue has maintained a consistency of style,* a consistent position in relation to naturalism.

Your plot should have allowed your major characters to change as a result of their experiences. Make sure that these *character developments are reflected in the dialogue* (again without necessarily being stated directly).

Make sure that *each character uses the speech patterns appropriate* for the individual and the situation, and that the *speech patterns of characters are sufficiently differentiated* from each other.

Make sure *you haven't unconsciously tidied up the language.*

Check that your dialogue is not too predictable. There ought to be a few surprises in there, but they need to be credible at the same time.

Make sure that *the dialogue engages us emotionally.* It may work in plot terms, or even in terms of development characterisation, but if it is not engaging us at an emotional level, it is not working.

If you have *a line that is only there to be funny, but isn't, cut it.*

Check that you are *not using words where action or visual effects would do the job better.*

Check that in the dialogue itself, *the ratio of telling to showing* is not unbalanced (remember that there should be a great deal more of the latter).

If you are using narration, make sure that you are not abusing it. Check that you are *not using narration to state the obvious, to provide a running commentary or just to fill in gaps.*

Make sure that *the dialogue doesn't allow tension to dissipate* where it should be building up. Any dialogue which is floppy, cut.

Check that the *presentation is correct.* Make sure that the layout is appropriate for the medium and that you haven't written unnecessary directions for the delivery of the lines.

So, there is a lot to be looking out for. And take care that when you alter something, you take into account the knock-on effect on other parts of the dialogue, or other elements of the script. A change in a line of dialogue may subtly alter characterisation, and this in turn may lead to another character responding to this one in a slightly different way – perhaps in a part of the script a considerable distance from the point where you made your initial alteration. Or a change in dialogue might release or hold back a piece of information, which perhaps has an effect on dramatic irony elsewhere. Even something as simple as changing a name can have unexpected results. If you decide, for example, that Kevin should become Anthony, it is easy to tell the computer to alter every occurrence of the name, but in fact the change alters the rhythm of the sentences. Our language is strongly rhythmic (we tend to speak in duple or triple rhythm), so where the name actually occurs in the speech, for the new sentences to run smoothly you might well find yourself having to add (or take out) little one-syllable filler words. (When changing names I now try to find names with the same number of syllables.) Do try to think through – and act on – *all* the implications of all your changes.

It is in fact very difficult to think through all the effects of alterations in advance. It is also hard simply to bear in mind all the aspects listed above at one sitting. Furthermore, while you are altering one part of the dialogue it is hard to *feel* the whole script, and how it is changing. For all these reasons it is a very good idea to leave another time gap and then read the script through again, making further adjustments. The process should be repeated as many times as necessary, until you are entirely happy with the result. *But each time, before you carry out changes, make a copy of each existing version.* You might find that you change your mind and want to revert to the previous version, so make sure you allow yourself that opportunity.

You Must Be Your Own Harshest Critic of Dialogue

Of course, others will have their own comments and suggestions about your dialogue, but you must first be a perfectionist. Once you have sent off the script, it may well be too late to be coming up with ideas of how this or that aspect of the dialogue could be improved. And don't always feel that tinkering is the answer. Be willing to take drastic action, cutting whole sections if necessary, and being willing to make major alterations to dialogue which will affect the script in all sorts of other ways. Remember that you always have the previous version(s) to go back to if you decide you want to. A timid approach can only produce limited improvements. *Be bold.*

14. Last Words

Don't think you've ever cracked it

Language is a living thing, so it is changing all the time. New words enter the dictionary (or at least come into use); words change their meanings or drop out of our lives entirely. New phrases appear, and new references from current affairs slip into the language. So dialogue – in real life and in scripts – changes too, and we have to keep abreast of it. Even social codes change, so that while we may be using the same words with roughly the same meanings, we may find ourselves using them in slightly different settings. Again, we must be sensitive to this: dialogue written to conform to the social codes of twenty years previously (perhaps the formative years of the writer) will not do.

So, *keep listening*. Keep listening to language as it is used by all sorts of people in all sorts of different situations. Play them back to yourself in your head. Analyse exactly what is going on – the use of vocabulary, the sub-texts, everything.

And *keep your eye out for artistic innovations*. Keep up to date. Listen to scripts on the radio, watch their realisation on television, film and the stage. Listen to scripted language critically, and if you like a new way of presenting dialogue, add it to your repertoire. This does not mean you imitate the dialogue of another writer, but simply that you learn from it. Miller didn't imitate the dialogue of Ibsen, nor Stoppard imitate that of Beckett, but they certainly learned from each other, and adapted their work for their own uses.

So enjoy spoken language. Take a delight in its enormous and minute variations. And enjoy your scripting of dialogue.

Index

180

181